NELL'S BELLES

The Swinging
Sixteen-Sixties Show

by Kjartan Poskitt

Copyright © 2002 by Kjartan Poskitt
All Rights Reserved

NELL'S BELLES is fully protected under the copyright laws of the British Commonwealth, including Canada, the United States of America, and all other countries of the Copyright Union. All rights, including professional and amateur stage productions, recitation, lecturing, public reading, motion picture, radio broadcasting, television, online/digital production, and the rights of translation into foreign languages are strictly reserved.

ISBN 978-0-573-08118-7

concordtheatricals.co.uk
concordtheatricals.com

FOR AMATEUR PRODUCTION ENQUIRIES

UNITED KINGDOM AND WORLD
EXCLUDING NORTH AMERICA
licensing@concordtheatricals.co.uk
020-7054-7298

Each title is subject to availability from Concord Theatricals,
depending upon country of performance.

CAUTION: Professional and amateur producers are hereby warned that *NELL'S BELLES* is subject to a licensing fee. The purchase, renting, lending or use of this book does not constitute a licence to perform this title(s), which licence must be obtained from the appropriate agent prior to any performance. Performance of this title(s) without a licence is a violation of copyright law and may subject the producer and/or presenter of such performances to penalties. Both amateurs and professionals considering a production are strongly advised to apply to the appropriate agent before starting rehearsals, advertising, or booking a theatre. A licensing fee must be paid whether the title is presented for charity or gain and whether or not admission is charged.

This work is published by Samuel French, an imprint of Concord Theatricals Ltd.

The Professional Rights in this play are controlled by Concord Theatricals, Aldwych House, 71-91 Aldwych, London, WC2B 4HN.

No one shall make any changes in this title for the purpose of production. No part of this book may be reproduced, stored in a retrieval system, scanned, uploaded, or transmitted in any form, by any means, now known or yet to be invented, including mechanical, electronic, digital, photocopying, recording, videotaping, or otherwise, without the prior written permission of the publisher. No one shall share this title, or part of this title, to any social media or file hosting websites.

The moral right of Kjartan Poskitt to be identified as author of this work has been asserted in accordance with Section 77 of the Copyright, Designs and Patents Act 1988.

USE OF COPYRIGHTED MUSIC

A licence issued by Concord Theatricals to perform this play does not include permission to use the incidental music specified in this publication. In the United Kingdom: Where the place of performance is already licensed by the PERFORMING RIGHT SOCIETY (PRS) a return of the music used must be made to them. If the place of performance is not so licensed then application should be made to PRS for Music (www.prsformusic.com). A separate and additional licence from PHONOGRAPHIC PERFORMANCE LTD (www.ppluk.com) may be needed whenever commercial recordings are used. Outside the United Kingdom: Please contact the appropriate music licensing authority in your territory for the rights to any incidental music.

USE OF COPYRIGHTED THIRD-PARTY MATERIALS

Licensees are solely responsible for obtaining formal written permission from copyright owners to use copyrighted third-party materials (e.g., artworks, logos) in the performance of this play and are strongly cautioned to do so. If no such permission is obtained by the licensee, then the licensee must use only original materials that the licensee owns and controls. Licensees are solely responsible and liable for clearances of all third-party copyrighted materials, and shall indemnify the copyright owners of the play(s) and their licensing agent, Concord Theatricals Ltd., against any costs, expenses, losses and liabilities arising from the use of such copyrighted third-party materials by licensees.

IMPORTANT BILLING AND CREDIT REQUIREMENTS

If you have obtained performance rights to this title, please refer to your licensing agreement for important billing and credit requirements.

NELL'S BELLES

Nell's Belles was first performed by Hexham Junior Youth Theatre at the Queen Elizabeth High School, Hexham, on 30th March 2001, with the following cast:

Nell Gwyn	Pip Neesham
Rose Gwyn	Rachel Oliver
Helena Gwyn	Alice Marples
Violet	Annie Eccles
Mercy	Sarah Norris
Agatha	Imogen Ogilvie
Annie	Laura Gittins
Bess	Jessica Cunningham
Charles Hart	Daniel Walton
Robert Duncan	Robbie Fergus
King Charles II	Joe Cowling
Queen Catherine	Molly Dunne
Barbara Villiers	Lucy Burton
Louise	Tessa Buchanan
Hortense	Georgina Mitchell
James	Warren Smith
Mr Chiffinch	Sam Roberts
Mrs Chiffinch	Eleanor Toolin-Kerr
Irene	Becky Powell
Rita	Rebecca Dixon
Elsie	Sally Bryant-Haswell
Tom Farrinor	Kalum Fergus
Titus Oates	Sarah Hogg
Duke of Buckingham	Henry Musto
Father Huddlestone	Patrick Doherty
Doctor	Daniel Walton
Nurse	Emily Dowden
Soldier 1	Chloe Graham
Soldier 2	Amy Livesey
Barmaid	Anna Kirk
Newspaper Seller 1	Laura Murphy
Newspaper Seller 2	Michael Turner
Newspaper Seller 3	Patrick Doherty
Newspaper Seller 4	Amy Livesey

Members of the Chorus: Rachel Barnes, Rebecca Best, Shani Fielding, Eve Gargett, Katie Hannant, Megan Held, Alexandra Holway, Meisha Holway, Emily l'Anson, Kathryn Maude, Lyndsey Rogan, Heather Runnacles-Goodridge, Sarah Scott, Anna Speed, Grace Towler, Lindsay Walton, Johanna Wild, Lucy Winter, Jack Young

Band leader, John McKillup
Designed by Toby Olie
Produced by Vivien Hubbuck and Lesley Silvera

CHARACTERS

Nell Gwyn, the actress
Rose Gwyn, her sister
Violet
Mercy the Belles
Agatha
Annie } the twins
Bess
Helena Gwyn, Nell's mother
Charles Hart, an actor
Robert Duncan, a theatre manager
King Charles II
Queen Catherine
Barbara Villiers, a mistress
Louise, a mistress
Hortense, a mistress
James, King Charles' brother
Mr Chiffinch, the Page of the Bedchamber
Mrs Chiffinch, Keeper of the Privy
Irene
Rita } Charlie's Charladies
Elsie
Tom Farrinor, the baker
Titus Oates
Duke of Buckingham
Father Huddlestone
Doctor
Nurse
Soldier 1
Soldier 2
Barmaid
Newspaper Seller 1
Newspaper Seller 2
Newspaper Seller 3
Newspaper Seller 4

Characters & Casting Notes

Vera
Pauline
Ivy
Brenda } extra charladies
Dot
Connie
The Reaper

Chorus including: **Singers, Girlfriends, Charladies, Guards, Ghosts**

CASTING NOTES

Nell's Belles was written particularily for companies which have more female performers than male. However, the balance of parts can be easily readressed by having men play some or all of the Charladies.

Many of the smaller roles can be doubled making the show suitable for fifteen performers or even less.

SYNOPSIS OF SCENES

ACT I

The Prologue. 1649: An Empty Street Near Tower Hill
1663 The Stage at the Drury Lane Theatre
The King's Bedroom Landing
Outside the Rose Tavern
The Magic Room
On the Stage at the Drury Lane Theatre
The Saloon of the Rose Tavern
News Stand
The Baker's Shop, Pudding Lane

ACT II

The Construction Site at St Paul's Cathedral
The King's Bedroom Landing
Nell's Dressing Room
The Palace Hallway
The Seaside
A Palace Corridor
Outside the Rose Tavern
Inside the Rose Tavern
The Palace Vaults
Outside the King's Bedroom. February 1685
Inside the King's Deathchamber
The Palace Gardens
The Sixties

MUSICAL NUMBERS

Song 1	**Happiest Days**	Full chorus
Song 2	**Palace of Love**	Charles, Chiffinches and Girls
Song 3	**A Little Bit of Bawdy**	Violet, Agatha and chorus
Song 4	**Cross my Palm with Silver**	Mercy, Annie, Bess
Song 5	**All Shut Out**	Nell and the Belles
Song 6	**The Reaper**	Agatha, Belles, Ghosts and Corpses
Song 7	**Charlie Boy**	Nell and the Belles
Song 8	**Fire!**	(Instrumental)

ACT II

Song 9	**The Phoenix**	James and full chorus
Song 10	**No Commitments**	Nell
Song 11	**The Seaside Special**	Belles and full chorus
Song 12	**Life Without You**	Charles and the Belles
Song 13	**Filth!**	The Charladies
Song 14	**Gimme the Nurse**	Catherine, Charles and Belles
Song 15	**Happiest Days (reprise)**	Company
Song 16	**The Seaside Revisited**	Company

A full Piano/Vocal score, which is suitable for rehearsals or performance is available from Samuel French Ltd.

Additional band parts for drums, bass, guitar and saxophone are available from the author via Samuel French Ltd.

A demonstration cassette of all the songs is available from Samuel French Ltd.

Recorded backing tracks suitable for use in productions are available from the author via Samuel French Ltd. These are best played from CD or Minidisc, but cassettes are also available. All tracks were written and recorded by Kjartan Poskitt with additional vocals by Josie Mills.

AUTHOR'S NOTES

Scenes, Changes and Charladies

Although there are several different scenes, they can all be played on the same basic set. The set should have two nondescript doors. During the course of the show names can be hung on the doors saying where they lead to.

Scene changes should only take a matter of seconds, all that is needed are minimal extra props and furniture, and signs hanging on the doors.

The scene changes are done by the Charladies, some of whom also take dramatic roles.

If your theatre has a front-cloth, then the directions in the text indicate which bits of the the action could take place in front of it. This would allow for more complicated sets to be assembled behind.

Cutting/Altering the text

The entire show runs to about 1 hour 50 minutes (excluding an interval). Please feel welcome to cut any songs or dialogue to make the show more suitable for your company, and do feel free to alter one or two lines to make funny topical or local references. However, please do *not* add extra dialogue, and do *not* put in other songs!

Further Production Notes

From time to time, updates and suggestions for the show will be posted on my website that also gives details of my other shows and some brief music demos that canbe played. If you have access to the internet visit www.kjartan.co.uk

Kjartan Poskitt

*Other musicals by Kjartan Poskitt
published by Samuel French Ltd*

Fawkes, the Quiet Guy
Henry, the Tudor Dude
The Rumpelstiltskin Racket
Sammy's Magic Garden

NELL'S BELLES

The sixties was an amazing time.
The war was finally over,
The government was relaxed,
The country was in a party mood and
The people had never had it so good.

No wonder the details are a bit hazy.

A lot of what follows actually happened.
Most of the rest probably happened.
As for the fine details —
Anyone who claims to know it all
Can't have been there.

ACKNOWLEDGEMENTS

I'd like to thank all the producers of my shows over the last years for their hard work, feedback and (when I can get there) hospitality! I'm especially grateful to those who cajoled me into writing *Nell's Belles* including: Terry Marsh, David and Margaret Carter, Caroline MacArthur, Marianne Shaw and finally Vivien and Lesley who were so keen to be the first producers that they came down from Hexham and banged on my door.

Kjartan Poskitt

For Bridget
and our own little Belles,
Maisie, Florence, Dulcie and Miranda

ACT I

THE PROLOGUE.
1649: An Empty Street Near Tower Hill

There is a slow beat of a single drum. A distant crowd murmurs

The Lights come up. If the theatre has a front-cloth then the following scene could be played in front

Two Puritan Soldiers enter, DS. It's cold. They shiver and stamp their feet as they address the audience

Soldier 1 Back you go, there's nothing to see.
Soldier 2 Hur hur! No, nothing at all. Just the last ever King of England having his head chopped off. Hur hur!

The Soldiers look offstage

Soldier 1 In case you're interested, old King Charlie's wearing two shirts.
Soldier 2 Bet you can't guess why.
Soldier 1 He doesn't want the cold to make him shiver. In case the crowd think he's nervous about being executed.
Soldier 2 Gotta admit, he's got style, that bloke.
Soldier 1 Style? He's a bloodsucking parasite feeding on the slavery of an impoverished nation.
Soldier 2 Yeah, but he's stylish with it.

Helena, drunk, slowly staggers on stage, clutching her head and holding a bottle. She sings to herself unsteadily

The Soldiers block her path

Helena (*singing*) Charlie boy, you're not to blame ...
Soldier 2 Hold it there, missus.
Soldier 1 Yeah and cut the singing out.
Soldier 2 Mr Cromwell's in charge now and he doesn't like singing or dancing or any of that stuff. From now on it's just going to be boring.
Soldier 1 Yeah, lovely and boring.
Soldier 2 I can't wait to get bored. Can you?

Soldier 1 No. I'm going to get bored right out of my mind every day. It'll be brilliant.
Soldier 2 Look! Bernard's got his axe up...
Soldier 1 Go on, Bernard!

The Soldiers move towards the exit to get a better view

Soldiers (*chanting*) Off in one! Off in one! Off in one ...

A few seconds later there is a huge cheer, as the king's severed head flies on to the stage and is accidentally caught by Helena. She doesn't realize at first what she's got. She clutches the hair with one hand and holds up the head to her face. She thinks hard, then still holding the head up with one hand, she gives the head a drink from her bottle. The liquid splashes to the floor. Slowly, she looks underneath and is amazed to realize there is no body. She feels the empty space where the body should be. She is utterly gobsmacked

The Soldiers return looking round

Soldier 2 Where did it go?
Soldier 1 Over here somewhere. Oh, look! She's got it.
Soldier 2 Sorry, love. Time to kiss your boyfriend goodbye, hur hur.

Helena kisses the head

Soldier 1 Oh, gross!

Helena clasps on to the head

Soldier 2 Now then, don't be difficult.
Soldier 1 His family want to stitch it back on to his body before they bury him.

Helena slowly relinquishes the head

Soldier 1 You'll go down in history, you will.
Soldier 2 Yes, the last woman ever to kiss a King of England. Hur hur.

The Soldiers exit, taking the head

Helena waves the head a sad little goodbye and stares amazed after them. She cannot comprehend what's just happened

A Barmaid enters

Act I 3

Barmaid Helena — there you are! We've been looking all over for you. What's been happening?
Helena There was a ... It flew over and then ... Oh, nothing much.
Barmaid Come on, you've got customers waiting.

Helena indicates the bottle

Helena You know this stuff that we sell to our gentlemen? We've got to put the price up. It's fantastic.

Helena and the Barmaid exit

The front-cloth rises or Black-out

        1663: THE STAGE AT THE DRURY LANE THEATRE

Song 1: Happiest Days

During the musical introduction, the Lights come up

It is a large bare stage. There are one or two theatrical items such as laundry baskets and odd boxes around. There are two doors. One door could be marked with a star and the other could just say "Wardrobe"

A big chorus of singers enters. The chorus includes Nell; Rose; Agatha; Violet; Twins, Annie and Bess, and Mercy — they are collectively referred to as the Belles. They all prepare to sing

All (*singing*)   Do you remember back in forty-nine?
                    We had a king who thought he was divine
                    They took him to court and they took off his head
                    That was the day that the world went dead
                    Holidays and happiness became a crime
                    Ev'ryone forgot there'd been a better time
                    But now we can dance, and now we can sing
                    Once again there's a bright new king
                    Kids of the Sixties
                    They'll never know
                    The gloom of the Fifties
                    So long ago
                    They tell us that we've never had it so good
                    They tell us that we've never had it so good
                    These are the happiest days of our lives.

Ev'ry single morning brings a better day
Ev'ry single dance'll blow the night away
Summer and autumn, winter and spring
Ev'ry day has a treasure to bring
Ev'ry body party till we hit the top
Nobody can tell us that we've got to stop
We're coming out like a shot from a gun
Young and single, ready for fun.

Kids of the Sixties
They'll never know
The gloom of the Fifties
So long ago
They tell us that we've never had it so good
They tell us that we've never had it so good
These are the happiest days of our lives.

Happiest days of our lives

Charles Hart and Robert Duncan enter through the auditorium and walk up on to the stage. Hart does flamboyant gestures with a large, bright distinctive handkerchief. Duncan carries some bits of paper and a notebook and pen

Duncan Jolly good! Well done.
Hart Next!
Rose Next? What do you mean "next"?
Violet Just a minute, Mr Big Posh Actor, sir. We've been practising our act all week.
Hart Act? We don't want an act, Duckie, we want an ac-*tress*.
Chorus An actress?
Violet What, just one?
Hart Just one. So, if you don't want to be an actress, then get out.

Rose holds back the other Belles — Nell, Agatha, Violet, Annie and Bess, and Mercy

The rest of the chorus goes

Rose We've come this far, we've got to give it a chance.
Nell I wouldn't mind being an actress.
Rose Let's all have a go.

There is general agreement from the Belles

Act I

Hart Oh, actresses are we now? Pah! This isn't some little sing-song! Darlings, this is *theatre*, and not just any little theatre but the Theatre Royal, Drury Lane.
Duncan We're planning the big opening night.
Rose We know that.
Violet We work round the corner at the Rose Tavern.
Hart The Rose! But that's a bawdy house! It's full of wanton women.
Violet Not today, it isn't. We're all here.
Hart You don't seriously expect us to put girls like you on stage, do you? Have you any idea who'll be out there?
Belles Charlie boy!

The Belles all make a swooning noise. Hart puts his handkerchief in his pocket out of sight

Hart "Charlie boy"?
Violet His Royal Highness King Charles the Second to you.
Rose Of course we know Charlie's coming! Our song's all about him.
Nell Yeah, about how boring life was with Oliver Cromwell ——
Rose — and how much better it is with Charlie boy.
Hart "Charlie boy"? Saints preserve us!
Duncan Well, I thought your song was great fun.
Mercy So would Charlie. He likes anything bawdy.
Hart How could you possibly know?

Twins, Annie and Bess usually speak in unison

Twins Everybody knows about Charlie!
Mercy You ask my mum. She was sneaked into the palace one night.
Twins Yeah, and our auntie's been.
Violet My granny went one night and took both her sisters.
Duncan Come on, Charles, let's give them a chance.

Rose approaches Hart and strokes his sleeve

Rose Yeah, that's all we want. A chance.
Violet We don't want to spend our whole lives dishing up brandy to ugly blokes.

Rose puts her arms around Hart

Rose Put us in your show.
Hart For the last time, we do not require a sing-song. Next!

Hart rejects Rose. Everyone looks off stage. Nobody comes on

Violet There isn't any next.
Duncan I may as well take their names, Charles.

Duncan prepares to write. The Belles form a line

Rose Rose and Nelly Gwyn.
Duncan Gwyn? Not Helena Gwyn's girls?
Nell That's us.
Duncan Their mother was the last girl ever to kiss the old king.
Hart He must have been off his head.
Nell Yeah, it was something like that. (*She chops the side of her neck with the edge of her hand*)
Duncan Is it true?
Rose So mum says, but sometimes — you know — she's a bit out of it.
Duncan Any special skills?
Nell Our Rose? I'd say she has!

Nell nudges Rose who pulls a handkerchief out of her pocket. It is identical to the one we saw Hart using earlier. Duncan laughs. Rose passes it to Hart who is appalled

Hart She's a dipper!
Nell But she gave it back.
Rose So that proves I'm honest.

Violet approaches Duncan

Duncan Next please.
Violet I'm Violet.
Duncan Special skills?
Violet Violence.
Duncan Violins? You play the violin?
Violet *Violence.*
Agatha She's dead handy if you get trouble.
Duncan Useful to know. Next please.
Mercy Mercy.
Duncan Special skills?

Mercy holds out some cards

Mercy Pick a card. With your left hand.

Act I

Duncan picks one and turns it over

Duncan Three of clubs.
Mercy Aha. Your efforts will be rewarded.
Duncan I hope so! This theatre is proving a nightmare to set up.
Mercy Drury Lane'll be the best in the world. Believe me.
Duncan I'll try! And who are you?
Agatha What have I got to say?
Violet Tell him your name, Agatha.
Agatha My name is Agatha. That's Ag-ath-a.
Duncan Yes, I think I got it.
Agatha Who are you?
Duncan Robert Duncan
Agatha Special skills?
Duncan I act and I direct a bit.
Agatha Very good. Next please.

Agatha has confused Duncan into forgetting what he's supposed to be doing. Violet ushers Agatha away

Mercy And these are the twins, Annie and Bess.
Duncan Any special skills?
Twins No, not a thing.
Duncan Nothing?
Twins Er ... Let me think ... no.
Duncan Do you always talk like that?
Twins Like what?
Rose You get used to it.
Violet I'll show you something funny.

Violet comes up behind Annie and tickles her ribs. Annie doesn't move, but Bess doubles up as if being tickled

Bess Get off!
Duncan Oh. So you can talk independently then?
Twins Of course we can. What do you think we are? Freaks?
Nell So what's this show you're giving Charlie then?
Duncan We're presenting "The Humorous Lieutenant".
Agatha Who's he?
Hart He? *He*? "The Humorous Lieutenant" is a play, you ignoramus! A masterpiece of comedy and characterization. Or it will be if we can find enough men to play the roles.
Rose Men? You said you wanted an actress.

Hart We've changed our minds.
Duncan No, we haven't. It's the latest thing, instead of having men dressed up to play the women's parts, I thought we'd try a woman for once.
Hart Oh, honestly, Robert. You can't have women dressed up as women. They'd look ridiculous. It's unnatural. Give me a man dressed up as a woman any day.
Belles Wooo!
Hart All right, that's it. If you're not going to be serious you can all get out. *Now*!

The Belles move to go, but Rose loiters

Rose Who gets to play the main part then? This "Humorous Lieutenant"?
Nell He'll have to be pretty good if he's doing it in front of the king.
Hart Pretty good? He's a comedy genius! (*He struts around proudly*)
Rose So, who is it?
Duncan Haven't you guessed?

The Belles are amazed to see Hart strutting around proudly

Belles Him?
Nell Oh, why not? Anyone can be funny. Tell a few jokes, drop your pants, blow a few raspberries. Come on, girls, let's go ...

The Belles move further towards the exit

Hart *Stop*!

The Belles all turn round

(*Exploding his words*) Jokes? Pants? Raspberries?

The Belles all fall about giggling

Nell See? That's all you need. Jokes, pants and raspberries and even *he's* funny.
Hart I was not being funny.
Rose Let's see what you really do then.
Violet Yeah, if you're so good let's see you do a bit.

Hart is slightly abashed

Hart No, no. Not now. I couldn't possibly.

Act I 9

Agatha Oh, go on. I've never seen a great actor before.
Nell Me neither. Not a *really* great actor. Go on, please.
Hart No.

Rose takes a snuff-box from her pocket

Rose I'll give you your snuff-box back.

Hart snatches it crossly

Hart No.
Twins Because you can't, can you?
Hart I can.
Nell Go on then.
Hart Er— It's not convenient.
Belles Oh, go on!
Hart Well, er, ah — I'm a little rusty ...
Belles Hooray!

They all dash back and sit around to face Hart

Hart Top of Act two. "The Humorous Lieutenant" — that's me — comes on from the prompt side. Now watch ... (*He moves to the side of the stage. After a pause, he walks across limping and clutching his head in an exaggerated fashion. He then stands still beaming at them*)
Rose Now what?
Hart I'm waiting for the laughter to subside.
Mercy What laughter?
Hart My dears, surely you noticed the walk?
Violet Was that supposed to be funny?
Agatha I thought he'd just wet himself.
Nell Me too. I felt sorry for him.
Hart Robert ...?
Duncan Don't panic, Charles. When you're in costume, it'll be more obvious, and you'll get that big laugh.
Hart Of course! Where would actors be without their costumes?
Rose In prison. You can't go prancing about in front of the king naked.
Violet My granny did. And both her sisters.

The Belles giggle

Hart Can we get on? The whole point of the scene is that the humorous lieutenant is back from the wars with a massive head wound. Blood pouring everywhere, and yet ...What is his first line?

Nell You haven't said it yet.
Hart I know! I'm just about to. Ahem ... (*He delivers the following line in the traditional big booming voice with massive gestures*) "Fie but how my boots do pinch!"

Hart waits for big laugh but doesn't get one

(*To Duncan*) They're not laughing.
Duncan (*explaining the joke to the Belles*) The joke is, his head is bleeding, but he moans about his feet.
Belles Oh.
Hart Do you see? Now, I'll do it again and you'll laugh.
Violet Forget it.
Nell You're awful.
Hart I'd like to see you do better.
Rose Go on, Nell, you show him.
Nell OK. What do I do?

Duncan passes her some bits of paper

Duncan There. Just read the lines.
Nell Me? I can't read.
Hart There! What use could she possibly be?

Duncan takes the bits of paper from her

Nell Just tell me what to say and I'll say it.
Hart Don't help her, Robert. If she really wants to be an actress, she should be able to improvise.
Nell Impro — what?
Hart You should be able to *feel* your part like I felt mine.
Agatha (*confused*) Is that what actors do? Stand there feeling their parts? They'd be better off prancing round naked.

The Belles giggle at Agatha's innocence

Violet Shhh!
Hart Well? We're all waiting, Miss Superstar actress.

Nell limps a bit just like Hart did

Nell (*acting*) Oh, look at me, back from the wars
Covered in bruises, gashes and sores
But just to be funny I walk with a limp
Only an actor could be such a wimp.

The Belles laugh and cheer

(*Pointedly at Hart*) Only an actor's pretentious brain
Would make a big joke about soldiers in pain.
So pardon me if I don't want to know
About you and your act and your sad little show.

The Belles all cheer. Nell takes a big bow as they all applaud. Duncan is amused

Hart *Go!* Go, get out all of you.
Violet Don't you worry, we're going.

The Belles go

Hart (*to Duncan*) What are you laughing at?
Duncan I dunno. She's got something that girl.
Hart What does she know of theatre?
Duncan Nothing, Charles, that's the point! The whole profession stinks of greasepaint and sweaty tights and that's why she's a breath of fresh air. The big theatrical voice and all the arm waving-stuff, it's so artificial, it's deadly.

Hart struts around crossly waving his arms

Hart You're saying I'm artificial?
Duncan I'm saying she's not.

Hart sighs. They chat as they start moving off to the side of the stage

Hart Robert, do you think I'm too old to learn from someone like her?
Duncan Of course not.
Hart It might be good to have her around.
Duncan On stage?
Hart God, no! We'd never know what she'd say next.
Duncan We could fix her up as an orange girl.
Hart Perfect! But do you think she'd accept?

The cheering Belles dash back on. Nell runs to Hart and hugs and kisses him

Duncan Yes, I think she accepts.

They all move towards the exit, as they leave Rose hands some money, a penknife and pocket-book to Hart

Rose In that case, here's your money back, here's your penknife, your pocket-book ...

They all go

Charladies come on. They include Rita, and Irene, their boss

The Charladies set the props for the next scene. They remove the theatrical items — the laundry basket and odd boxes. They change the signs on the doors. One door has a crown-shaped sign reading, "Charlie's room" The other door has a sign on a string reading " Do Not Disturb." This sign is heart-shaped on the back and reads "Barbara's room", unseen as yet

During the scene change, Irene becomes aware that the audience are watching them

Irene (*to the audience*) What are you smirking at? Surprised to see a few Charladies up here, are you? Well you just wait till the filth starts. Filthy, that's what this show is, in't it, Rita?
Rita Filthy.
Irene Oh, we have our work cut out before the end, don't you worry. Right, are we all done?

Rita and the other Charladies go

Irene (*announcing*) King's bedroom exterior circa sixteen sixty-two.

Irene goes

The King's Bedroom Landing

Mr and Mrs Chiffinch enter with a tray of tea cups. They tap on the door marked "Charlie's room". They always talk like a radio double act

Chiffinch Hi! It's nine a.m. on a beautiful Tuesday morning, and once again it's your very own Page of the Royal Bedchamber and his wife ——
Mrs Chiffinch Hi!

Act I

Chiffinch — welcoming you to a brand new day!
Mrs Chiffinch Yes, indeed, the forecast's bright with showers expected later, so come on, Charlie, let's get moving, let's get grooving ...
Chiffinch Right! It's time to open that door and see what's hot and what's not.

Chiffinch taps on the door and it opens slightly

Song 2: Palace of Love

As the intro to the following song plays, exhausted girls in disarray emerge one by one. They are each handed a cup of tea. The girls look absolutely beat. Each new girl that enters could do a small "faint" on the word "ooh!" They all sing

Mr Chiffinch **Mrs Chiffinch** **Girls**	Doo-be dooby doo-wah — ooh! Doo-be dooby doo-wah — ooh! Doo-be dooby doo-wah — ooh! Doo-be dooby doo-wah Doo-be dooby doo-wah — ooh! Doo-be dooby doo-wah — ooh! Doo-be dooby doo-wah — ooh! Doo-be dooby doo-wah

Finally Charles bounds in waving a tennis racket. He has the traditional beard of the time. He sings

Charles	To see me is to sigh ...
Mr Chiffinch **Mrs Chiffinch** **Girls**	Is to sigh, is to sigh
Charles	And put the twinkle ——
All	— in your eye
Charles	So, come and let your——
All	— senses fly
Charles	In the palace of love...
Mr Chiffinnch **Mrs Chiffinch** **Girls**	In the palace of love
Charles	To hold me is to know...
Mr Chiffinch **Mrs Chiffinch** **Girls**	Is to know, is to know

Charles	You never want to——
All	— let me (him) go
	So come and let your feelings show
	In the palace of love
Charles	I don't mind admittin'
	When the book of love was written
	The picture on the cover — that was me.
	When I encounter beauty
	I respect my duty
	To give myself with generosity
All	So if you want a little fling
	Tap the door or give the bell a ring.
Charles	For a personal service from the king
All	In the palace of love
Charles	You're looking like you disapprove
	But even if I tried to move
	Wherever I go, there's girls at my feet
	Climbing in the windows, queuing down the street
	What's a guy supposed to do
	When you're king they want the most of you
	So I share myself round, I try to be fair
	A little bit here and ——
Mr Chiffinch ⎫ **Mrs Chiffinch** ⎭	— a little bit there
Girl 1	And a little bit there
Girl 2	And a little bit there
Girl 3	And there ...
Charles	And if you start presumin'
	There can't be enough room in
	My little heart for everyone plus you.
	Don't worry, it's fantastic
	It's made of strong elastic
All	So in you come and bring your sister too.
	If you want a little fling
	Tap the door or give the bell a ring.
	For a personal service from the king
	In the palace of love
	Palace of love

Act I

Irene, the Charlady comes in, with her mop and bucket. She holds the mop with the head uppermost

Irene Are you done in there?
Charles Hey! Who's this gorgeous creature?
Irene Who are you talking to? Me or my mop?
Charles I'll take both.
Irene Gerroff.

Irene goes out through "Charlie's room" door

Girl 1 Oh no! The queen's coming!
Girl 2 We better go!
Charles Why?

The Queen comes on. She's been hunting and has a bow and arrow

The girls all try to scarper but Charles stops them

Charles Hi, Catherine, babe!
Queen Hallo, Charles.
Charles Say hallo, girls.

The girls are creeping off past Catherine. Catherine is slightly irritated

Girls *(sheepishly)* Goodbye.

The girls exit

Queen Had a good night, did you?
Charles Now then, Catherine, we've been through all this before. I'm the king, and so everybody wants a piece. It's my job to dispense myself fairly and with generosity.
Queen Honestly, Charlie! You know I don't mind, but do try to be more discreet.
Charles Discreet? But I'm trying to set a good example! After all the miserable years under Cromwell, it's time for a bit of live and let live. I mean look at us. Me an English Protestant king, and you, you're Catholic and your brother's the King of Portugal. What a crazy mix-up and yet we're married. Isn't it just groovy?

Charles strokes the Queen's face affectionately. She likes it

Queen Oh, I suppose as arranged marriages go, it's not too bad.

Charles Not too bad? You're having a fab time! Before you came over here, you only ever went out once a year and that was to light candles in churches. Now look at you!

During the following, the Queen aims her bow and arrow at Charles

You dance all over town, you gamble my money away at cards and ... Don't you point that thing at me!

The Queen lowers the bow and arrow

Queen Charlie, the problem is that I'm the queen and you're the king. You want all the Catholics and Protestants in this country to get on together, don't you?
Charles Absolutely. Peace and love, man.
Queen Then it starts in here with you and me. If people think you're messing me about, then you're going to upset the Catholics, and there's a lot of us about. Even your little brother's turning Catholic.
Charles You mean James?

James dashes on

James I heard my name! What's happened?
Charles Nothing.
James Oh. I just thought you might be dying.
Charles Not yet. We'll let you know.
James Because I don't mind being king you know. I'll do a great job.
Charles *We'll let you know.*

James goes off

Queen He's strange that one.
Charles Hey, I love him! He's a great guy. OK, maybe he's a bit square when it comes to games involving blindfolds and bananas, but that's my brother. We're one big happy family.

The Queen rubs her stomach sadly

Queen I wish the family could be slightly bigger.
Charles Yeah, me too.
Queen The whole plan was for me to provide an heir to your throne. That way Portugal, England, Catholics, Protestants — it would keep everyone happy.

Act I

Charles You're not to worry about it. Sure we'll keep trying, but if anything happens to me, there's always James.

James dashes on

James I heard my name! What is it?
Charles ⎫
Queen ⎬ *(together)* Nothing!
James Well, I'll stay here in case you want me.

James goes to lean by the side of the stage. A small hand-bell tinkles off stage

Irene comes on from "Charlie's room" with her mop and bucket. She sees James

Irene *(shouting)* Oi! Hands off. I just polished that.

James hurriedly steps away as the hand-bell tinkles again

James *(trying to lecture Irene)* Now listen here, you ...

Irene ignores him

Irene *(shouting off)* Rita! Elsie! She's up and moving.
James I expect a bit more rexpect ... I mean rexpect more expect, respect. I mean respect more expect ...

Rita and Elsie — two more Charladies — come on with mops and buckets, barging James aside

James tries to face up to them

Elsie Out the way, you.
James I could be king any day now.
Rita King? I'll flippin' crown you myself if you leave footprints on my clean tiles.

Rita shoos James off stage. The bell tinkles again

James goes

Irene *(apologizing to Charles)* Sorry, boss. This is the big one. I'll finish your room later.

Charles Can't you do it now?
Irene Are you kidding? Not with Big Babs tinkling away.
Queen "Big Babs"?

The bell tinkles angrily. Rita laughs to Irene drily

Rita He hasn't told her, has he?
Queen Told me what?
Charladies Go on, tell her!
Queen Charles, who is ringing that bell?
Charles No idea.

The Charladies start to go off through the second door marked with "Do Not Disturb"

Charladies (*calling off*) Good-morning, Mrs Villiers.

They go

Queen (*furiously*) I thought I told you to move her out!
Charles Catherine, be reasonable! I can't send her home, it's the third time I've got her pregnant. Her husband would be furious.

Charles realizes he's just really put his foot in it. The Queen aims her bow at Charle's head and draws back the arrow

Whoa — let's be cool about this. Of course I can understand why you might be feeling just a little hassled, but we can talk this through. Please, not the face ...

The Queen lowers the bow to point at his groin

Oh, no! Not that. Honestly. Please ...

Charles runs off

The Queen goes to the edge of the stage then fires the bow off after Charles. We hear a distant scream from Charles

Barbara, very pregnant, comes on through the door marked "Do Not Disturb". She is dressed to go out. During the following, she turns the "Do Not Disturb" sign round to reveal the heart-shaped sign saying "Barbara's room"

Act I 19

Barbara Do you mind keeping the noise down!
Queen How dare you? I think you'd better leave.
Barbara Well think again. I've been with Charles a lot longer than you. I'm the one he takes everywhere, I'm the one having his children. Where does that leave you?
Queen I am his wife.
Barbara Wife? You sweet old fashioned thing! You're just an inconvenient political arrangement.

Barbara goes

The Queen is extremely upset

Irene, Elsie and Rita come on from the "Barbara's room" door. Elsie is carrying a chamber pot (containing confetti, unseen as yet)

Irene All done.
Elsie My God, but she can fill a chamber pot, that woman.
Queen Go away.
Rita (*sarcastically*) Charming.
Irene (*sensitive to the Queen's distress*) Hey, Elsie, wouldn't it be a pity if that pot accidentally fell all over Big Babs' specially imported feather mattress?

The Queen stares in surprise at Irene. Elsie and Rita are staring into the pot

Rita There's a few big Babs in here.
Elsie Funny how some float and some sink, isn't it?

The Queen decides to take advantage of having someone to talk to

Queen I wish I knew what to do. Whether to stay with Charles or whether to return to Portugal. If only I knew what was to happen.
Irene You ought to see a fortune teller.
Queen Why?
Irene They can tell your future.
Rita Then you can decide what to do.
Queen It sounds like witchcraft.
Rita Nah!
Irene They just look at your palm or some of them read tea leaves in the bottom of a cup.
Elsie I bet there's some that could tell Big Babs' fortune from this pot.
Queen Don't be ridiculous.

Irene People can do all kinds of things, like talking to dogs or making plants grow. As it happens, my sister's girl can read your fortune from a pack of cards. She's no witch.
Queen It doesn't sound right.
Irene Well, if you don't want to bump into her, you best avoid the Rose Tavern by Drury Lane.
Queen I'll avoid it.
Irene But if you do go there by accident, don't ask for Mercy Jones.
Queen Mercy Jones. I won't.

The Queen turns to go, but Elsie indicates the pot

Elsie So does the feather mattress get it?
Rita We'll blame it on the cat.
Queen Thank you, but that won't solve anything.
Elsie Aw!
Irene You heard her Majesty, so make sure you dispose of it in the usual responsible manner.

The Queen goes off

If necessary more Charladies can come on to start changing the scene during the following. They remove the signs on the doors and place a "Rose Tavern" pub sign next to one door

Rita I'll open the window. (*She walks to the front of the stage and mimes opening a window*)

Elsie stands behind her starting to swing the pot

Elsie Watch out below ...

Elsie chucks the contents of the pot on the audience. It's the confetti (of course)

All the Charladies go

Act I

OUTSIDE THE ROSE TAVERN

Violet, Agatha and the girl chorus come on

Song 3: A Little Bit of Bawdy

The song can either all be sung in unison or the main chorus can be divided into two sections A and B as indicated

Violet **Agatha**	(*chanting*)Come inside. Come inside Doors unlocked and open wide Whatever you want we can provide so Come inside. Come inside
Chorus A	(*singing*)Life can be lonely With nowhere to go Nothing to do and With no-one you know
All	So don't just wait, come and join the party It's not too late the evening has barely started
Chorus A	A little bit of brandy, that's all right
Chorus B	A little bit of bawdy makes your night
Chorus A	A little bit of brandy warms the blood
Chorus B	A little bit of bawdy does you good
Chorus A	Hallo, sailor, what you say? You'll find we have our uses.
Chorus B	Hallo, soldier, shoulders back, walk this way and excuses
All	A little bit of brandy, that's all right A little bit of bawdy makes your night A little bit of brandy warms the blood A little bit of bawdy does you good
Chorus B	Whatever your problem, Whatever your fear Step right inside And they all disappear
Violet **Agatha**	You've got trouble?
All	We'll help you forget it Come in at the double

Violet **Agatha**	Guaranteed you won't regret it
Chorus A	A little bit of brandy, that's all right
Chorus B	A little bit of bawdy makes your night
Chorus A	A little bit of brandy warms the blood
Chorus B	A little bit of bawdy does you good

All (*chanting*) Come inside. Come inside
Doors unlocked and open wide
Whatever you want we can provide so
Come inside. Come inside
A little bit of brandy, that's all right
A little bit of bawdy makes your night
A little bit of brandy warms the blood
A little bit of bawdy
Little bit of bawdy
Little bit of bawdy
If you can afford it
A little bit of bawdy does you good

The Chorus and Violet go

Agatha is left on duty by the Tavern Door

Violet comes out of the Tavern door dragging a man. Helena follows looking a bit the worse for wear

Violet Come on, you!
Agatha What's he been up to?
Violet He's smashed a chair, he's been sick on the cat, and he groped the Twins.
Agatha So what's the problem?
Violet He's run out of money.
Helena Another satisfied customer.

Agatha helps Violet thow the man off stage

The man goes

Agatha (*calling sweetly after him*) Have a nice day now.

Helena sniffs deeply

Helena Ah! There's nothing to wake you up like the smell of fresh sewage. You two can go for a wander if you like. I'll watch the door.

Helena stands unsteadily by the second door

Violet Are you sure you're up to it?
Helena Don't be cheeky. I was watching this door before you were even born.
Violet Helena ...

Violet indicates the Tavern door. Helena looks at it in confusion

Helena Fancy that! All these years I've spent at the Rose Tavern, and I never knew there was another one next door.
Agatha (*confused*) Is there really?
Violet Come on, Aggs.

Violet takes Agatha off. As they leave the Queen comes on. She wears a crown but the hood of her cloak is over it

Helena wanders back to the Tavern door

Helena (*calling*) Rose Tavern, right this way. Walk in and crawl out.

The Queen approaches

Queen Is this the Rose Tavern?
Helena Sorry, love, we've got enough girls. You'll have to find a job somewhere else.
Queen I'm looking for Mercy Jones.
Helena Oh. What's that under your hood?
Queen I don't know what you mean.
Helena You're wearing a spiky hat.
Queen Can I see Mercy Jones?
Helena Maybe. Can I see your hat?

The Queen glances round nervously then lifts her hood back to reveal her crown

Queen There!
Helena That is a pretty thing. I wouldn't mind one of those myself. I expect it stops the pigeons landing on your head when you're flat out in the gutter, doesn't it?

Queen May I go in?
Helena Oh, yes. In you go, love. First floor, straight ahead. Make sure you step over the puddles.

The Queen puts her hood up and goes through the Tavern door

(*Calling*) Bawdiest house in town. Guaranteed money back if you're not shocked and disgusted.

Violet and Agatha run back

Violet Helena — did you see her?
Helena Who?
Violet There's a state carriage at the end of the mews. A woman just got out and came this way.
Helena Ah! The spiky hat woman.
Agatha Spiky hat?
Helena For keeping the pigeons off. She wanted to see Mercy.
Violet You know who that was, don't you?
Agatha It's obvious. It's some woman who invents hats.
Violet Quick, Aggs, get up the back stairs. Tell Mercy the Queen's coming.
Agatha (*with disappointment*) The Queen? Aw! I always wanted to meet a hat inventor.
Violet *Go!*

Mercy dashes off

Helena It can't be the Queen. Why would the Queen need a hat to keep the pigeons off her head?

Violet ushers Helena off

Black-out

The Magic Room

When the Lights come up, there is a table with a long table-cloth which reaches the floor. There might also be oil lamps and candles for atmosphere. It all looks quite spooky

Mercy is sitting at the table with a deck of cards ready. Annie and Bess stand behind her. Rose, if possible Nell and Violet, and a fourth person sit underneath the table unseen by the audience

Act I

The Queen enters through one of the doors, leaving it open

Queen Mercy Jones?
Twins Come in. She's been expecting you.

The Queen turns back towards the door but it closes by itself

Song 4: Cross my Palm with Silver

Mercy (*singing*)	Cross my palm with silver and see what I know
	Many have before you and glad they did so
	From heads of principalities to theatre personalities
	They say how primeval it is but still have a go.
Twins	She can find your darkest deeds and bring them into light
	She knows all the nasty dreams that wake you in the night
	She knows on your shoulder there's a pink birthmark
	And knows who'll win the three o'clock at Kempton Park
Mercy	Cross my palm with silver and hear what I see
	Good or bad you get it with full guarantee
	So don't tell me that I'm a twister taking cash hand over fist, ah
	No, you're thinking of my sister
	Gypsy Rose Lee
Twins	She can tell you anything no matter how uncanny
Mercy	I could hold a conversation with your granny's granny's granny
Twins	She could get an answer from a head stuck on a spike
Mercy	So ask me anything you want I'll tell you what you like.

Instrumental

The table rises mysteriously into the air — (Rose and the other people under the table are responsible) — and other odd phenomena happen

The Queen is amazed. She passes a few coins over. During the last verse she shuffles the pack

Mercy	Cross my palm with silver then believe what you're told
	Shuffle the pack and your life will unfold
	If you find you start to wonder
Twins	Does she ever make a blunder
Mercy	Cast your doubts and fears asunder …
All	And behold!

Mercy Cut the pack, left hand please.

The Queen cuts the pack. Mercy takes the top card and sets it aside face down. She then starts laying some of the other cards out on the table, face down

Queen I've come about my friend.
Mercy That's a pity. You shuffled them, so the cards tell me about you.
Queen Not my friend?

Mercy picks up the face down card and looks at it

Mercy Four of spades. That means a lonely dark-haired woman.

The Queen tries to pull her hood a bit closer around her head. Mercy turns a card over — the nine of clubs

> Please — it's only a few cards. And you've got the nine of clubs which is money. A rich marriage perhaps? Or luck in gambling? Maybe both — your Majesty.

The Queen is surprised

Queen Money is not happiness.

Mercy turns up the queen of hearts

Mercy No, it isn't. But here's the queen of hearts.
Queen That must be good.
Mercy Hmmm. I'm not sure who she is yet but ...

Mercy turns up the queen of spades

> Oh dear — queen of spades.

Queen What's that?
Mercy It's your rival. Some other woman upsetting your marriage.

The Queen gasps

> Sorry. I just say what I see.

Queen She lies around under my own roof purring like a cat and breeding like a pig. She treats my husband as a toy, orders my own servants about. They call her Big Babs. I would kill her ...

Mercy turns a card — the ten of diamonds — and reacts happily

Mercy The ten of diamonds! So that's who the queen of hearts is!
Queen Who?
Mercy You are going to get a special friend. Someone who can help.
Queen Help get rid of the Babs woman?
Mercy I hope so… (*She turns up the queen of diamonds*) Oh.
Queen What now?
Mercy I've never seen that before. A third queen, diamonds. I'm afraid there might be more Babs women.
Queen More? Then that settles it. I'll get the Portugese ambassador, the very next boat he takes me home.

Mercy turns another card — the five of hearts

Mercy No.
Queen What do you mean, no?
Mercy I don't see a journey. This is better. The five of hearts is reconciliation.
Queen You mean, I win my husband back?
Mercy Let's see the last card. (*She turns the last card — the nine of hearts — and smiles*) The nine of hearts. Luck and friendship! It's the best card to finish on.
Queen Why?
Mercy The worst is behind you.
Queen Do you know what the worst is? When my husband walks in public, she is on his arm while I must find my own amusements. She laughs in my face, she jokes with strangers.
Mercy It won't last much longer.
Queen You sound very sure.
Twins She is.
Queen Very well. I'll suffer it a bit longer, but please, it must be secret that I came here. If the Babs woman ever knew, then I would just die.
Mercy Only the four of us will ever know.
Twins You can trust us.

The Queen is about to leave

Agatha rushes in

Agatha Mercy, I've got a message from Violet! You'll never guess who she is — she's the Queen! Sorry, I'm late, I've been telling everybody.

The Queen storms out

Twins Nice one, Aggs.

Mercy calls out and taps on the table

Mercy OK, she's gone!

Rose comes out from under the table. Nell and Violet come on from the side or from under the table. They've all obviously been listening

Agatha Wasn't I supposed to tell about the Queen?
Mercy Don't worry, Aggs. No-one ever believes you.
Twins They think you're mad.
Nell Queen or not, I don't half feel sorry for her.
Rose Yeah. This might not be much of a life, but hers sounds awful. Who is this Babs woman anyway?
Mercy Barbara Villiers. That woman Charlie always takes round with him.
Twins Oh *her*! She's revolting.
Violet I know who you mean. Why don't I just go up to her and smash her face in?
Agatha That's a really really good idea.
Mercy Come off it. Big Babs is not worth being arrested for.
Violet Shame. It'd be good to do something.
Mercy It would need to be something personal.
Nell Hey! Tomorrow night — at the theatre! Charlie's coming, he's bound to bring her.
Rose So?
Nell Maybe we could sort her out and get ourselves out of this place.
Belles How?
Nell We're *all* going to be orange girls! Come on.

The Belles go off

Irene and the Charladies come on to prepare the next scene. This involves putting a "royal box" DS at the side or in the auditorium

The other Charladies, other than Irene, go off

Irene (*announcing*) Drury Lane Theatre circa 1664. (*As she makes her way to the exit she whistles at the table*) Come on. Back to your cupboard.

The table follows Irene off stage. (The fourth hidden person operates the table)

Black-out or the front-cloth falls

Nell and the other Belles enter the auditorium

Act I

ON THE STAGE OF THE DRURY LANE THEATRE

As the Lights come up DS, *Nell and the girls are walking around the front of the auditorium. Each has a basket of oranges*

Belles (*generally shouting*) Oranges! Get your oranges! If you can't stand the show don't just sit there, chuck something ...

There is a fanfare and a cheer

   Charles enters the royal box

Violet He's here!
Rose But has he brought her?

There is some booing

Heavily pregnant Barbara joins Charles in the box. She is wearing a feather boa. She tries to wave at the audience

The booing increases. Barbara looks away haughtily

Violet Maybe I should just hit her.
Nell Rose, get me that boa! And anything else.

Song 5: All Shut Out

Nell gets on stage

Rose walks up to the King and hands him an orange. He takes it gladly. Barbara turns away in a huff so Rose deftly removes her boa and tosses it to Nell

Barbara That boa's just like mine!
Charles Shhh. I'm watching!

During the first verse of the following song, Rose also gets Barbara's fan and possibly other stuff such as her necklace and so on. She passes it on to Nell

   The other Belles sneak off

Nell (*singing*)	I'm trying not to try too hard
	I'm desperate to show I don't care
	But as soon as my eye spots a reas'nable guy
	I find that my pride, has crawled off and died

And then the old devil inside me
Takes control of my brain
I come on like fool, I act distinctly uncool
And I'm all shut out again.

The other Belles and girl chorus come on to the stage behind Nell. They all have pregnancies and feather boas like Barbara's

Chorus I'm only trying to show that I'm friendly
Any time of night or the day
I don't hurt anyone but still they all run
Like it's a crime to have a good time
I wish I could say I don't need them
I know that they're not worth the pain
But still I give chase and they laugh in my face
And I'm all shut out again.
Oh why... do I...
Make such a fool of myself
Oh, why do I ....
Put on a dress, try to impress,
Work to excess, look like a mess
And all the time they couldn't care less
And I end up on the shelf

Nell I want to be the heart of the party.
I want to be the belle of the ball
Chorus But somehow I'm stuck always having to look
Like a wet fish in search of a hook
I wish that I could play the old hard to get
That way drive them insane
But no I can't ignore them, I over-adore them
Then I'm all shut out
All cut out
In no uncertain terms I'm told to butt out
Yes I'm all shut out again.

Big cheer

Barbara runs off

There are shouts of derision

Hart comes on

Act I

Hart What is going on here?
Charles Encore! Marvellous!
Hart Your Majesty, I can't apologize enough. (*To Nell*) You, you're fired.
Charles What for?
Hart Embarrassing your companion, sire!
Charles It was a joke! Barbara's far too uptight. To be honest, she's getting a bit heavy, starting to be a bit of drag, you know what I mean? But I really dig that chick, she's fun. What's your name?
Nell Nell Gwyn, your Majesty.
Charles And what do you call your lovely friends?
Nell This is Rose, and then Violet, Agatha and the Twins ...
Charles Ooh! Too complicated. I'll just call them Nell's lovely friends. How does that sound?
Belles Brilliant.
Charles Yes, brilliant. Nell's lovely friends. No actually it's awful, isn't it?
Belles Awful.
Charles Nell's Beauties. How's that?
Belles Even brillianter.
Charles Listen, I've been thinking about having a do out near Oxford. How'd you like to sing for me there?
Belles Brilliant.
Charles It's going to be a giant sixties peace and love festival at this place called Woodstock.

The Belles all leap about

Belles (*chanting happily*) We're going to Woodstock — we're going to Woodstock.
Charles We could have a big sign up saying "Woodstock Festival starring Nell's Beauties"? What do you think?
Belles Brilliant.
Charles Actually now I think about it, no, it's not going to work. Sorry. I've changed my mind.

All the Belles are completely crestfallen. They turn away and slowly move towards the exit

Rose So much for our big chance.

Charles has not realized the upset he has caused

Charles (*after a brief think*) Got it! A big sign saying "Nell's Belles!"
Belles Eh?

Charles That's what we'll call you! "Woodstock Festival starring 'Nell's Belles'". So, are you on for it? Say "Yes, Charlie".

The Belles are ecstatic

Belles Yes, Charlie!
Charles It's a date then!

Charles gets up to leave

Hart But sire, you haven't see the play yet.
Charles Haven't I? Is it any good?
Hart Sire, it is a masterpiece of theatrical extemporization, honed to perfection ...
Charles Great. Well do let me know how it goes. (*He moves towards the exit but turns back*) Here's to "Nell's Belles!" (*He blows them a kiss*)

The Belles all swoon

"Nell's Belles." You've got to admit, that name has a certain ring to it.

Charles goes

Hart Bah!
Rose Never mind, Mr Hart.
Violet Come on, we'll take you down the Rose Tavern.
Twins (*together*) We can do you something special.
Hart Thank you, but no.
Violet Please yourself ...

The Belles, apart from Nell, go

Nell Sorry he never waited to see your acting.
Hart He's seen me before. I'm sure he preferred your song.
Nell It was just a song. It's not like I've ever had any training or anything.
Hart Well make sure you never do.
Nell Why not?
Hart Because I was supposed to be the big star tonight, but it was you.
Nell And so you hate me. Fair enough.
Hart It doesn't quite work like that. In fact I'd be honoured if you'd let me take you out to dinner.
Nell Take me out to dinner? You mean you're going to pay for mine as well as yours?

Hart Yes please. I want to talk about putting you on the stage properly.
Nell Wow! You talk, I'll listen.

Hart and Nell join arm in arm and are about to go off

The other Belles all stick their heads round the corner

Belles Wooo!

Nell flicks them a cheeky sign or blows them a raspberry as she and Hart go off laughing

The front-cloth rises or the Lights come up US

Irene enters. (If necessary other Charladies come on with tables and chairs to set the scene)

THE SALOON OF THE ROSE TAVERN

Irene (*anouncing*) The Rose Tavern interior, February 1665.

Irene and the Charladies go

The Belles enter and sit round practising

Rose Let's try it once more — two three.

Nell sings. The other Belles sing an "Ooh" backing

Nell Charlie Boy, look my way
Just the merest smile from you's enough to make my day...
(*Speaking*) Is it sounding better?
Rose Not bad, but Woodstock's only a couple of weeks away.
Twins I'm a bit nervous.
Violet Oh it's not much different to being down the Rose. We give them a bit of a song and a laugh. Are you OK, Aggs?

Agatha is looking very unwell

Agatha I'm a bit shivery.
Rose We all are. It's just nerves, that's all. Once we're singing we'll be fine.
Nell What do the cards say, Mercy?
Mercy (*taking the cards from her pocket*) You cut them, Nell. Left hand.

Nell cuts the pack. Mercy deals out. Violet feels Agatha's forehead

Violet Your head's hot, Aggs. And you're sweating like a pig.
Rose Never mind. If this concert goes well, we might be playing the palace next! Think of the crowds and the money we'd make
Nell So are we going to get rich, Mercy?

Mercy turns the first card — two of spades. She looks puzzled

Mercy Eh? I can't see what it's trying to tell us.
Nell What do you mean?
Mercy Two of spades. It means something bad or unlucky.
Nell So this concert is going to be a waste of time.
Mercy I don't think it's the concert, but I need another card.

Agatha is collapsing

Violet Hey, Bess, Annie, get over here. She's falling. (*She goes to help Agatha*)

The Twins rush to help Violet. Mercy shuffles the cards anxiously

Nell You look worried, Mercy.

The Twins scream and show Violet, Agatha's neck

Twins Look at her neck!
Violet They look like some sort of love bites.
Rose Love bites? *Agatha?* (*She goes over to Agatha*) No! I've seen those marks before. Remember when she found those two French sailors in the gutter down Drury Lane?
Violet They died, a right horrible death too!
Rose They had the same marks.

Mercy fans the cards out for Nell to pick one

Mercy Go on, Nell.

Nell takes a card and hands it to Mercy face down. Agatha starts convulsing. The Twins try and hold her. Violet loosens Agatha's top

Twins What's happening?
Violet Oh, God! It's right down to her armpits! It's the plague!

Mercy turns the card up

Mercy The nine of spades. We've got DEATH!

The Lights dim and it gets spooky for fantasy sequence

> *A "Grim Reaper" figure in a black cowl comes on ringing a bell. Other spooky figures wheel on a cart with some corpses on it*

Agatha suddenly awakens and regards the Ghouls with curiosity

Song 6: The Reaper

Agatha (*singing*)	I can hear a bell!
The Reaper	Bring out your dead!
Agatha	Someone's calling for me.
Rose	She's delirious!
Violet	Agatha! There are no voices! There's nothing there!
The Reaper	Your time has come.
Agatha	I've got to go!

Agatha turns to move towards the Reaper's cart but the others implore her not to go

All	One step towards us, hold out your hand
	Don't look behind you it's the *Reaper*
	Don't start to weaken, keep up your stand
	Don't be a victim of the *Reaper*
	He's gonna throw you on the devil's pyre
	And set your soul on fire
	You're gonna burn burn burn
	Burn burn burn
	Burn burn burn
	Whoa ....
	Reaper!
	Don't go a riding with the
	Reaper!
	Don't go a riding with the
	Reaper!
	Don't go a riding with the
	Reaper!
	Don't go a riding ...

The Corpses suddenly all sing nicely

Corpses	He's going to take us somewhere far away
	Where ev'ryone is happy, skies are never grey
	If you're feeing cold and tired
	And pain fills your inside
	Just step aboard and take a ride...
All	No...! No...! No...! No...!

Short instrumental

> One step towards us, hold out your hand
> Don't look behind you it's the *Reaper*
> Don't start to weaken, keep up your stand
> Don't be a victim of the *Reaper*
> He's gonna turn your ashes into lime
> Until the end of time
> You're gonna burn burn burn
> Burn burn burn
> Burn burn burn
> Whoa ...
> *Reaper!*
> Don't go a riding with the
> *Reaper!*
> Don't go a riding with the
> *Reaper!*
> Don't go a riding with the
> *Reaper!*
> Don't go a riding ...

Agatha	When I look back, and see what became of me
	I was always young and happy, that's what I wanted to be.
	But with this fever now I've turned from young to old.
	I want the fire to kill the cold
All	No...! No...! No...! No...!

Short instrumental

> One step towards us, hold out your hand
> Don't look behind you it's the
> *Reaper*
> Think of your fam'ly, think of your friends
> Think of Charlie ...

Agatha Charlie?

Act I 37

There is a sudden final chord

The Reaper, Ghouls and Corpses all exit

Agatha returns to where she was lying when the song started. The Belles are all round her

The Lights returns to normal

Agatha stirs

Agatha What happened to the Woodstock concert?
Rose It got cancelled.
Violet You've been out of it for a month, Aggs.
Agatha I've ruined it for you all.
Nell Don't be silly. If anything's to blame, it's the plague.
Twins (*together*) They say it might get worse.

Hart comes in

Hart Nell!
Girls Oooh, it's lover boy!
Hart You haven't got this plague thing have you?
Nell Me? Not so far.
Hart That's good because my friend Johnny Dryden's written a new play "The Indian Emperor". There's a leading role for you although it's a bit serious.
Mercy Nell? Serious?

For the rest of the scene all the Belles have a good laugh at Nell's expense

Rose (*teasing*) Oh dwarling, Eleanor, I caught your little play. Duckie, you were simply divine.
Nell You're joking, aren't you?
Hart This plague has scared all the straight actresses out of town.
Nell Oh. So I'm not exactly your first choice.
Hart If you can do this well and impress Johnny, he'll write something specially for you.
Rose What's the point writing for her when she can't read?
Nell Shut up, Rose. The Twins can read. You'll help me, won't you?
Twins (*together*) Of course, dwarling. (*They do mock "air kissing"*) Mwoi, mwoi.
Mercy (*outrageously camp*) And trust little me to buff up all your hats and cozzies, sweetie.

Agatha I'll shave your legs.
Nell Oh stop it!
Hart Come on, we're meeting at the theatre.
Rose Yes, go, Nell! And know in your heart that all our hopes and dreams go with you.
Nell Will you shut up!

Nell starts to walk off with Hart. Violet steps to walk in front of them like a body guard, pretending to brush people out of the way

Violet Clear a way there. Get back from the red carpet, *big* star coming through. No autographs please, Miss Gwyn is now leaving the building ...

The Belles all jeer and laugh

Nell (*turning crossly to Hart*) Now, look what you've started.

Hart and Nell leave with the giggling Belles all following and shouting stuff like "Nelly, darling, you look fabulous" "We love you, Nell" "Give us your autograph" etc...

Charladies enter quietly

The front-cloth falls

If there isn't a front-cloth the Charladies could quietly change the scene US, *to a "Baker's shop", while the "News Stand" scene is played in front. They change the bar to a baker's counter and remove the stool and drinks, etc. They set some lit candles. When the scene is set the Charladies exit*

The Lights come up DS

NEWS STAND

The Chiffinches enter reading some glossy Stage magazine

Mrs Chiffinch What a fabulous life style these stars lead.
Chiffinch (*reading*)"West End crowds flock to greet theatre's new golden couple".
Mrs Chiffinch (*reading*) "Nell Gwyn and Charles Hart dazzle with their chemistry, both on stage and off!"
Chiffinch (*reading*) "Before their last standing ovation had died away, their coach had whisked them from the stage door to a secret rendezvous."

Mrs Chiffinch It seems like nothing could possibly go wrong for them ...

They both turn to the audience grinning

Mr Chiffinch ⎫
Mrs Chiffinch ⎬ (*together*) Or could it?

A Newspaper Seller comes on, with some newspapers to sell

Seller 1 (*shouting*) Read all about it! All theatres to close as plague spreads right across London.
Chiffinch Well, isn't that a pity?
Mrs Chiffinch Yes, oh deary me. Just when Nell Gwyn was starting to be famous.

Newspaper Seller 2 comes on, with some newspapers to sell

Seller 2 (*shouting*) Stop press! Dozens dying in the gutter of mystery continental illness.

Newspaper Seller 3 comes on, with some newspapers to sell

The Newpaper Sellers start trying to out-do each other

Seller 3 (*shouting*) Get the latest. Streets littered with hundreds dying in agony.
Seller 2 Hundreds?
Seller 3 Yeah, hundreds.
Seller 2 I've only got dozens.
Seller 3 Tough! I've got hundreds.

Newspaper Seller 4 comes on, with some newspapers to sell

Seller 4 (*shouting*) Late edition! Pestilential Peril: thousands perish.
Sellers 1,2,3 Thousands?
Seller 3 He's only got dozens.
Seller 4 I've got thousands. What's more I've got "rats attack humans even as they lie screaming in the street."

As the following symptoms are read out, Seller 1 acts out each one

Seller 2 Aha! But I've got the official plague symptoms guide. (*Shouting*) Official symptoms include violent shivering!

Sellers 3 That's nothing. (*Shouting*) Victims ache all over with agony!
Seller 2 (*shouting*) Victims drown in streams of their own sweat.
Seller 3 (*shouting*) Victims vomit themselves to death!
Seller 2 (*shouting*) Big ugly lumps grow round your neck and armpits ...
Seller 3 (*shouting*) And in your groin.
Seller 4 Feeble! Listen to this. (*Shouting*) Victims rip their own faces apart in mad convulsions
Seller 2 You always have to go one better, don't you?
Seller 3 Yeah, you just made that up.
Seller 4 See for yourself.

Seller 4 indicates Seller 1 who is rolling on the floor attacking himself. Seller 1 suddenly stops dead

Mrs Chiffinch He won't be needing this then. (*She takes the paper from Seller 1*)

The other Sellers drag Seller 1 off

Oh, look Chiffy, here's a handy tip. If you get the plague, before you die, why not brighten up your front door by painting a nice red cross on it?
Chiffinch Super — red's my favourite colour.
Mrs Chiffinch And more good news! Even though the final death toll is projected to be around eighty thousand, at least your ravaged body won't go floating off into space.
Chiffinch Hey! Why's that?
Mrs Chiffinch Because Isaac Newton has just discovered gravity.
Chiffinch Bless him! A few months back it was the Binomial theorem, now Gravity, but do you know the one I'm really waiting for?
Mrs Chiffinch What's that, Chiff?
Chiffinch Differential calculus.
Chiffinch
Mrs Chiffinch (*together*) Gurr...oovy!

Mr and Mrs Chiffinch go

The front-cloth rises or the Lights fade to Black-out

Act I

THE BAKER'S SHOP, PUDDING LANE.

As the Lights come up, the Belles come in. Mercy is holding a note

Twins Hallo? Hallo!
Violet Are you sure this is the place?
Mercy Farrinor's Bakery, Pudding Lane. This is the place.
Nell It's funny coming back to London after the plague, isn't it?
Rose What's funny is getting that note asking us to come here.
Violet Hallo! Anyone in?

The Baker comes in with a tray of pies and other eats

Baker Aha! Ladies, sorry to keep you. I was just getting the nibbles out of the oven. I expect you fancy something tasty, don't you? Eh? *Eh*? (*He does a very unsubtle wink*)
Violet Who are you?
Baker Me? I'm Tom. Now there's wine and ale in the pantry and I'm going out. So I'm leaving you to it, know what I mean? Eh? (*He winks again*)
Rose What exactly is this about?
Baker Didn't he say?
Rose Didn't who say?
Mercy We just got this note.

The Baker looks at it

Baker (*reading*) "Tom Farrinor's bakery" — that's me all right. He'll be along soon, then you'll be all right too, won't you, eh?
Belles *Who*?
Baker You mean you don't know? Well, if he hasn't signed it, maybe he wants to surprise you, know what I mean? Eh? *Eh*?

The Baker winks and goes

Rose wolf-whistles him as he goes past

Agatha I don't like this.
Twins It's a bit creepy.
Violet Yeah, but that food smells good.
Rose A good-looking bloke that can cook. I can't believe I let him go.

Mercy suddenly straightens. She has sensed something

Mercy Someone's coming!
Violet Stay back you lot.

Charles comes in, wearing an identical false beard over his real beard. He looks round to see if he's being followed

Charles Sorry, I'm late!

Violet holds his throat and pins him against the wall

Violet All right, matey. What's your game?
Charles Put me down! Please, it's Agatha, isn't it? Or Rose?
Nell He sounds like Charlie.

Violet releases him

Violet He doesn't look like Charlie.

Charles pulls his false beard away showing his real beard

Charles There.
Girls Charlie!
Charles Charlie? Is that what you call me?
Girls Sorry, your Majesty.
Charles I prefer "Charlie".

Violet is staring at her hands in amazement

Violet Oh, my God! I was strangling the king.
Charles It's my fault. I didn't want to be recognized sneaking out.
Violet I'll never wash my hands again as long as I live.

Charles creeps up behind Bess, grabs her waist and kisses her neck. Bess hardly reacts but Annie squeals with delight

Charles I just can't help doing that.
Nell What are you doing here?
Charles I need a bit of fun. And if I remember rightly, fun is what you girls are good at.
Rose So why are we in a baker's shop?

Charles There are too many eyes and ears in the palace, and besides the queen's had a hard time of late. I'm trying to be more discreet. Tom's been a friend for years, he can keep a secret. Well come on, is anyone going to get me a drink?

The Belles bustle round to offer the King a drink and some of the Baker's food

Agatha Are you really the king?
Charles Too right, babe. You girls, make sure you help yourselves. I feel I ought to make it up to you.
Nell Make what up to us?
Charles The Woodstock concert not working out. I like to keep my promises.
Violet The plague was hardly your fault.
Charles You'd be surprised. When you're king, everything's your fault.

The King sighs tiredly. The Belles are concerned

Nell Are you all right? Really?
Charles I'll survive, it's just the last few months have been a bit heavy.
Nell What, with the plague?
Charles There's the plague and the war with Holland, but the biggest problem is trying to stop all our Catholics and Protestants killing each other. I'm stuck in the middle trying to keep them apart. Do me a favour, let's change the subject. So, have you got any new songs?
Nell Songs?
Charles What were you going to do at Woodstock?
Rose Go on, Nell!
Nell Now?
Charles Not like you to be shy!
Rose You always wanted to sing for the king.
Nell But ... Well, it's a bit hard, just singing right at his face.
Charles I could go back a bit.

Mercy indicates the auditorium

Mercy Good idea. Go right back there.

Charles makes his way to sit with the audience. A spotlight could come up on Charles

Rose There, Nell. Now just pretend you're on stage in front of thousands of people all staring at you.

Nell I'll try.

Nell calls out at Charles as if addressing a stadium

Nell Hallo, Woodstock!
Charles Hallo.
Nell Is everybody feeling *all right*!
Charles Yes, thank you.
Nell Then let's do it!

Song 7: Charlie Boy

Nell sings and the other Belles do the backing vocals

	Charlie boy, look my way
	Just the merest smile from you's enough to make my day
	Though you'll never see
	What you mean to me
	Charlie boy
	In the dark of the night
	I dream of you and suddenly my whole world comes alight
	Although you're not there
	I've learnt not to care
	Charlie boy...
Belles	Oh, Charlie boy
Nell / **Rose** / **Mercy**	Other guys they make their eyes at me And tell me that I'm hoping in vain
Belles	Tell me that I'm hoping in vain
Nell / **Rose** / **Mercy**	But I'm not the sort to drink water While I'm still dreaming of drinking champagne
Nell	Charlie boy, I can wait
	A week, a month, a year or more, you'll never be too late
	I won't interfere but I'll always be here
	Charlie boy ...
Belles	Oh, Charlie boy
Nell / **Annie** / **Bess**	When I work, when I play When I sing and when I sew and when I pray

Nell	Ev'ry hour of the day I'm waiting for you
	Charlie boy
Nell ⎫	When I laugh, when I weep
Annie ⎬	When I'm waking up or dropping off to sleep
Bess ⎭	
Nell	Maybe I'm mad, but I've got it bad
	Charlie boy …
Belles	Oh, Charlie boy
Violet ⎫	Other guys they all despise her pride
Agatha ⎭	And say she's set her target too high
Belles	Say she's rather set her target too high
Nell	But I'd never wish for what's under my feet
	I'd rather wish for the stars in the sky
	Charlie boy, I can wait
	A week, a month, a year or more, you'll never be too late
	I won't interfere but I'll always be here
	Charlie boy...
Belles	Oh, Charlie, Charlie my boy.

Charles claps

Charles That's a nice song, Nell. Where did you get it?
Nell It's a bit like the song my mum used to sing about your father.
Rose But Nell made it better.
Nell We all did.
Charles Well, this Charlie boy is very touched. Very touched indeed. You lot are wasted in a tavern, I promise I'll see what I can do. I want everyone to hear your singing. Especially you, Nell.
Nell Glad you liked it.

Charles makes his way back to the stage. Fade spotlight, if it has been used. He sidles up to Nell. He only has eyes for her and Nell is rather excited

The other Belles and girl chorus start to creep off behind Charle's back. They are greatly amused at Nell's predicament and make coarse signs and letcherous pouts at Nell. Nell tries to wave them away

Charles I wish I could write songs, Nell.
Nell Oh, it's easy.
Charles Then show me, Nell. Show me how to make real music. Just you and me baby, let's harmonize.

All the girls are horrified at this naff line. They all tickle their throats and pretend to throw up

Nell If you don't mind my saying, your Majesty...
Charles Charlie.
Nell I mean, Charlie, that's a really gross chat up line. "Show me how to make real music!"
Charles It usually works. I thought it was a winner. So, what's a better line?
Nell (*hissing at the girls*) Just go, will you?
Charles "Just go, will you"?
Nell No, not you.
Charles For goodness sake, Nell! What's this line I'm suppose to use? Open Sesame?

The girls all stifle laughter. Nell makes a final gesture to the girls

The girls go

Nell Honestly, Charlie! You're the king! All you need to say to anyone is: "I'm the king. How about it?"
Charles Oh. Well how about it?
Nell You got it!

Charles scoops Nell up and carries her off. As they go they knock over a candle. Off stage, Nell shrieks and giggles

The candle sets off a fire. The stage is lit with flickering orange and there is a smoke effect if possible

No: 8 Fire!

Instrumental Act I finale

For comic effect during the music, the Charladies could come on with fire helmets and fire extinguishers

Black-out

ACT II

The Lights come up on the construction site at St Paul's Cathedral

A congregation of people are singing with James at the front. There is a big empty seat

Song 9: The Phoenix

The music starts with the "Fire!" theme that finished Act I. However this intro moves into the introductory chords of the song.

All Like the Phoenix from the flame
The spires of London rise again
Bigger bolder stronger than before
Even as the last smoke clears
A greater city now appears
Built in stone to last for ever more
Gone are rotten timbers
And crumbling walls of mud
All replaced with
Mortar bricks and steel
Built on new foundations
Of stone instead of wood
What was once a vision
Will soon be here for real
So to God we offer thanks
For giving London such a chance
To grow bigger bolder stronger
Higher wider longer than before.

Charles enters and takes the empty seat just before the end of the song

Charles Has it started?
James Started? It's just finished. Where have you been?
Charles Busy! So how was the show?
James The show? This is the consecration service for the new foundations of St Paul's Cathedral. You should have been here on time.

Charles Hmmm, this place is a bit too Catholicy for me. It's more your lot than mine.

The Belles sneak in behind them

James Oh, no! Have you still got those girls staying with you?
Charles Those girls are hot stuff.
James Hot stuff? You're not kidding. Thanks to them you burnt down most of London.
Charles Me? What makes you think that?
James I know about the baker's shop in Pudding Lane.
Charles Baker's shop?
James Tom Farrinor's place. Everyone knows that's where the fire started, and I know you were there. A few drinks, a few girls, somebody gets careless ...
Charles Shut up, James.
James Do you know what it's going to cost? This new Cathedral alone will be seven hundred and twenty-two thousand, seven hundred and ninety-nine pounds, three shillings, one penny and one farthing.
Charles Some days you scare me, you know that?
James *You* scare *me*! The money for rebuilding London should have gone on the navy. It's in a terrible state. In fact there's nothing to stop the Dutch sailing up the Thames and moving in.
Charles Moving in where? It's all burnt down. See? You worry too much.
James Charles, thirteen people died in the fire! It's a miracle it wasn't more, so will you cut the Merry Monarch bit? This is serious.

Charles realizes that James needs a serious talking to

Charles OK, if you want "serious". I'll give you serious. Of course, it's tragic that thirteen people died, but the real miracle is that the fire got rid of the rats and so got rid of the plague. The fire probably saved thousands of lives.
James Oh! So the fire was a good thing was it? Then I'll tell everybody how it started shall I?
Charles Don't be mad. There would be a civil war and my head would end up on a spike.
James Hey cool! Then I'd be king.
Charles James this is *war*! Not a game of pass-the-parcel with the crown in it. Trust me, your head would be on the spike next to mine.
James It's so unfair. I could miss my chance of being king because of you.
Charles Not so long as you keep your mouth shut.
James You can rely on me, but what about this gaggle?

Act II

Charles I trust them a lot more than I trust you.
James I bet you don't even know their names.
Charles I do! There's Nell of course, then there's Agnes, er ... Vera ... um ...
James Get rid of them. Get them out of Whitehall, get them out of your life. That way even if they do talk, no-one will believe them. They must not be seen with you.
Charles They're my friends and I promised to help them become singers...
James Singers? They're a threat to national security! You might want your head on a spike but I don't. Ditch them, Charles. Go on, do it!
Charles If you insist.

Charles turns his back to the audience and speaks to the Belles. He crosses his fingers behind his back

Sorry, girls. I'm not allowed to see you any more.
Belles What?
James Are you all listening?
Belles Yes.

During the following as Charles continues, James walks to the side. Charles turns sideways and shows the Belles he has his fingers crossed. The Belles point this out to each other excitedly

Charles Sorry, I won't be able to help you with your lives, but I hope it works out for you all. And, Nell, if you get some more acting to do I'll try and pop in to watch but that's it. No meetings afterwards, and definitely no you-know-what. On no account are you to come to Whitehall palace on Fridays after you've finished work. And you certainly don't go to the second floor and make your way to the last room on the right.
Nell I wouldn't dream of it.
Charles There, James. Satisfied?
James Yes.
Charles That's it then, girls. So, goodbye for ever.

Charles walks off

James turns round to face the girls

James So, get back to wherever you came from. I command you.
Agatha I don't like him.

Titus Oates comes on

Titus That man is the king's brother!
James See? I'm famous.
Titus The Catholic convert.
James Yup.
Titus Burn him I say!
James What?
Titus A just revenge for the fire of London! Burn him!
James But, but ...
Titus Everyone knows the great fire was a Catholic plot, so burn him like the heretic he is.
James (*panicking*) I didn't start the fire.
Agatha Did he?
Violet Now I come to think of it, I saw him!
Mercy Me too.
Twins We saw you!
James What? No, I never! Not me ...

The Belles all shout at James

Twins Murderer!
Violet They'll hang you!
Agatha I don't like you one bit.

James runs off

Titus is very smug and starts sermonizing, but the Belles don't listen to him

Titus Yes, friends, think on this: who started the fire? It was the Catholics!
Agatha Has Charlie really dumped us?
Mercy No. We just have to keep a low profile for a while.
Titus Listen to me: who started the plague? The Catholics!
Violet Do you think he will come and see you, Nell?
Nell I dunno, but I feel worse for you lot. At least I've got some acting coming up, what will you all do?
Rose Well the first thing we'll do is go and have a party.
Violet What?
Mercy But we haven't any money.

Rose produces a purse from her pocket

Rose Oh, we've got some. Old James might find he's a bit light though.

They are about to go off in high spirits, but Titus accosts them

Act II

Titus So we must destroy the Catholics before they destroy us ...
Violet Out of the way, Nutter.
Titus Deny me would you? But of course, you are the king's foreign floozies! All shameless Catholics!
Rose Wrong! We're English and proud of it.
Titus Prove it!

All seven Belles turn around and flash their pants. They are wearing either union Jack undies, or they are in line with the letters E-N-G-L-A-N-D across their rears. (This is an artistic interpretation of a real event)

Titus runs off shielding his eyes. The Belles have a huge laugh and go off

Irene, Elsie and Rita, the Charladies, come on with a selection of brushes and buckets. They put the signs on the doors: one of the doors has a crown shaped sign reading "Charlie's room". The other has a heart-shaped sign reading "Barbara's room". They remove the chair

The Charladies stay on stage mopping

Irene (*announcing*) The king's bedroom landing in the late sixteen sixties. Sit up and concentrate because this is the tricky bit.

THE KING'S BEDROOM LANDING

Mrs Chiffinch runs on with a showbiz magazine and meets Mr Chiffinch coming the other way. They ogle the magazine

Mrs Chiffinch Look at this! It's outrageous.
Chiffinch Disgusting!
Mrs Chiffinch I can't look.
Chiffinch Ever since the theatres re-opened after the fire, that Nell Gwyn's got ruder and ruder.
Mrs Chiffinch Look at this one: "Secret Love" by John Dryden.
Chiffinch "Miss Gwyn's costume is almost non-existent. And it was specially commissioned by her biggest fan, the king."
Mrs Chiffinch The king? But I thought he was supposed to be keeping away from her!
Charladies AHA!
Chiffinch Do you know something we don't?

During the following, the Charladies describe everything with mops and brushes representing the different people. They use dusters to indicate the king's crown and other props accordingly

Irene *(to audience)* Are you ready for this? Off you go then, Elsie.
Elsie The king is married to Catherine, right?
Mr Chiffinch ⎫ *(together)* Right.
Mrs Chiffinch ⎭
Irene *(indicating Rita)* But ——
Rita — her job's to be the queen, so usually himself sees somebody else when he needs a seeing to, right?
Chiffinch Right.
Rita And so for the past few years he's been seeing a lot of Big Barbara Villiers ——
Irene ⎫ *(together)* — and there's a lot of her to see ...
Elsie ⎭
Rita And thanks to her services to the crown, he made Big Babs the Duchess of Cleveland, right?
Chiffinch ⎫ *(together)* Right.
Mrs Chiffinch ⎭
Rita But being Duchess got her bossing folk around and sticking her nose in all over and so himself starts getting a bit bored of her. So —— *(indicating Irene)*
Irene — that's why he asks you two to arrange a bit of variety now and then.
Chiffinch *(horrified)* How can you possibly know that?
Charladies Because we're Charladies!
Irene You'd be amazed how many different ankles we trip over on a morning.
Rita So there you are getting other people to see to the king, which of course means Big Babs isn't getting seen to herself, so she starts seeing who else is on the scene. Right?
Chiffinch ⎫ *(together)* Right.
Mrs Chiffinch ⎭
Elsie Meanwhile our Nelly has been seeing the actor Charles Hart, right?
Chiffinch ⎫ *(together)* Not the king?
Mrs Chiffinch ⎭
Elsie Well ——
Irene — himself is supposedly seeing a lot of another actress Mall Davis, but who really knows what goes on behind the scenes, eh?
Chiffinch ⎫ *(together)* Right.
Mrs Chiffinch ⎭

Irene is jiggling all the mops together to suggest a lot of complicated bawdy going on. Elsie picks up a couple of buckets to indicate the Dutch navy and Rita has a bucket to be the "Royal Charles"

Irene *(indicating Elsie)* But ——

Act II

Elsie — if everybody's busy seeing to each other, they're not paying attention are they? So while they're otherwise occupied, the Dutch navy come sailing right up the Thames ——
Rita — and they pinch the *Royal Charles*.

Elsie and Rita enact this with the buckets

Chiffinch They pinched him?
Mrs Chiffinch What? Like they pinched him on the bottom while he was — you know ...
Rita No! The *Royal Charles* is a boat and the Dutch pinched it.
Elsie Pay attention, can't you?
Chiffinch So how does that affect anything?
Irene The *Royal Charles* was himself's very favourite boat, and he was so upset that he shut all the theatres down. That meant neither Nell nor Charles Hart had any wages coming in. Right?
Chiffinch
Mrs Chiffinch } (*together*) Right.
Irene Well, you can't live on nothing, so Nell went off looking for a bit of rich stuff and she finished up seeing Lord Buckhurst who keeps her in Epsom ——
All Charladies — where everybody drinks the salty water.
Chiffinch
Mrs Chiffinch } (*together*) Right.
Irene (*indicating Rita*) But ——
Rita — with Nell gone, that meant Charles Hart was free so guess who turned up on his doorstep looking desperate?
Chiffinch
Mrs Chiffinch } (*together*) Big Babs.
All Charladies Big Babs indeed.
Irene In the meantime, thanks to Mall Davis, himself gets a taste for actresses, and suddenly Lord Buckhurst is packed off to France for no reason. That means that Nell doesn't have to get straight home after work anymore and ——

"Charlie's Room" door opens and Nell comes on. Charles looks round the door brushing his teeth

Nell See you later, Charlie!
Charles Shh! You'll wake up Barbara.
Nell Is she in there?
Charles She hasn't had a better offer for weeks.
Nell Oooh — she'll be in a foul mood!

Charles Shhh! Bye, Nell.

The Queen comes on from the side and walks across

Charles Morning, Catherine.
Queen Morning, Charles. Morning, Nell.

Charles goes back inside

Queen I loved the show last night.
Nell Thank you, your Majesty. Did those flowers arrive in the royal box for you?
Queen You shouldn't have!
Nell It was so nice that you came to see me.
Queen I wouldn't have missed it for the world.
Nell Well, got to dash. Goodbye!
Queen Hang on! (*Calling out*) Oh, Barbara! Nell's just leaving. Did you want to say goodbye?

Barbara looks out of her room in a foul temper and sees Nell

Nell Hi, Barbara. Sleep well?
Barbara Barghh.

Barbara goes back in

The Queen is delighted

Queen See you, Nell!
Nell Bye!

Nell and the Queen go off in different directions

The Charladies gather their equipment up

Irene So, there we have it. One big happy family. All right girls, scene change time.

During the following, the Charladies change the scene to Nell's Theatre dressing-room. This could involve bringing on a couple of dressing-room chairs, a mirror, and changing the door signs to stars

Chiffinch (*to the audience*) Ladies and gentlemen — we have just moved from 1666 to 1669 which involves some of the most complicated domestic arrangements in history.

Act II   55

Mrs Chiffinch (*to the audience*) So before they go, a big round of applause for the people who explained it so clearly...
Chiffs Let's hear it for Charlie's Charladies ...

Pause for applause for the Charladies

Irene (*announcing*) A non-specific theatre dressing-room, November 1669.

They all leave

NELL'S DRESSING-ROOM

Helena and Mercy enter and wait in the dressing-room

We hear applause

Nell comes on, wearing a hat. She looks tired and slumps into a chair

Mercy helps remove her hat, brings her a drink and generally helps her

Mercy Well done, Nell!
Helena She's such a star! I can't believe how far she's come since she was born.
Nell It's not that far, Mum. You had me in the Drury Lane coal-yard, remember?
Helena Did I? Still, that's never put Charlie off you, has it? Mind, come to think of it, he hasn't been in for weeks, has he?
Nell Leave it, Mum.
Helena (*to Mercy*) Aw! She's missing him, you know.
Mercy Feeling sick?
Nell It's not too bad.
Helena Sick, eh? It must be love!
Nell No, it isn't, Mum.
Helena How do you know?
Nell How do any of us know?

Song 10: No Commitments

(*Singing*)   I don't think it's love, it's just a funny feeling
               When I'm with him I could walk along the ceiling
               I know I keep his handkerchief in my pocket
               I even have a clip of his hair in my locket
               But I don't think it's love 'cos I've never told him

How much it means to have him and hold him
I get by fine when I know he's elsewhere
We're happy as friends so we're leaving it there

No commitments either side
No promises to break
We share good times just for good times' sake

No lost tempers no red eyes
We just live for the day
So love would only spoil things anyway
And suppose it was so, how would I know?
I've never been in love before
What should I feel if I thought it was real?
It all sounds a bit of a bore.
'Cos, I'm having fun and I don't care who knows it
This is my life and it's just as I chose it
What I hear of love, it's too complicated
With headaches and heartaches it's well over-rated

No commitments either side
No promises to break
We share good times just for good times' sake

No, lost tempers no red eyes
We just live for the day
So love would only spoil things anyway

Helena Well love or not, it must be something special between you two. You've even got your own rooms in the palace.

Nell Mum, let me try and explain about Charlie. He's been married to Queen Catherine for eight years now.

Helena Pah! That was just an arrangement.

Nell Look, if you must know, they're desperate for a son but it just isn't working. They try to be cheerful about it, they have parties and holidays together, but it isn't easy. There's times when she's been ill, he's kicked all the doctors out and sat with her himself. He sits up all night if he has to.

Helena (*impressed*) Never! Does he? Imagine a man doing all that for you.

Mercy You don't look so good, Nell.

Nell I'm all right.

Helena No, you're not. If he can nurse the queen, why can't he nurse you? It's unfair.

Mercy Unfair! Are you going to tell her, Nell?

Helena Tell me what?
Nell You tell her, Mercy.
Mercy What's unfair is that the queen is so desperate to give Charlie a boy and yet Nell's the one that's expecting.
Helena What? Have you had a pregnancy test?
Nell Mercy did it yesterday.
Mercy Seven of hearts, ace of spades and three of clubs reversed. Need I say more?
Helena My little Nelly's hit the jackpot!
Nell I beg your pardon?
Helena King Charles always lays out money on his kids.
Nell No, thank you. I don't want to be like Barbara. She's got four of Charlie's kids and she's always demanding money and titles for them. The queen's in tears about it.
Helena You make sure you get something, even if it's just for the baby.
Nell Not if it upsets the queen.

Charles taps on the door and enters

Helena stares at him accusingly

Nell Charlie!
Charles Hallo, Nell! Come here you ... (*He gives Nell a kiss; he notices Helena's stare*) What's up with your mother? OK. I know I missed the show but I've had to do some king stuff. Honest! It's a secret treaty with France. I promise to become Catholic, they give me some money and a few French places, then we all go and beat the Dutch up and I get my boat back.

A dead pause

What? Is it something I said? It's only the French for goodness sake! Once I've got the dosh, they can all go jump in the channel and we can party, party, party!
Helena She's having your baby.
Charles Nell! Fantabulous! I love babies, babies are just the best.
Nell The queen will hate me.
Charles Hate you? Never! Nell, listen: would you want to be queen?
Nell Me? I would *not*.
Charles And that's why you'll always be welcome. There's plenty of others trying to steal Catherine's place, there's plots all over Europe to replace her so I can have a Catholic son, you're the only one who isn't trying to use us, Nell. You make us laugh. So is it going to be a boy?

They all turn to look at Mercy

Mercy I don't know! How can you tell that from a pregnancy test?

Black-out

All exit

The front-cloth falls

THE PALACE HALLWAY

The Lights come up

Two doors are marked with "Charlie's room" and "Barbara's room"

Mr and Mrs Chiffinch come on checking clipboards

Chiffinch The scene's really swinging down at the palace, so let's catch up on who's hot and who's not!
Mrs Chiffinch And the big news is that Barbara Villiers is finally on the way out.
Chiffinch So who will be the king's new official favourite?
Mrs Chiffinch Nell must be a contender along with the new baby...
Chiffinch But no, it seems that Barbara is going to be replaced by the French government.
Mrs Chiffinch What? All of them? How many beds will we need?
Chiffinch No! There's a plan being arranged by the Duke of Buckingham to bring a French girl into the palace, so let's catch the action.

The Duke of Buckingham and Louise come on. He carries a suitcase

Charles comes on

Duke Hey, Charlie! Look what I brought you back from Paris. She was over here last year.
Charles Of course! Hi! It's Linda, isn't it?
Louise Louise Rene de Penancoet actually.
Charles See? I was close.
Duke Rather gorgeous, isn't she?
Charles And I bet she's got a beautiful personality.
Louise So which is my room?
Charles Room? Already? That's tricky because the queen's at the end of the corridor and Barbara's in here ...
Louise (*indicating another direction*) So who's down there?

Charles Little Charlie of course! You've got to see him!

Charles clicks his fingers

  Agatha comes on with a baby

Charles There's my boy and — look! He's got little bootees! Awww!
Agatha I hope you don't mind. I made them myself.
Charles They are just *so* cool. You're a star, Agatha.
Agatha (*blushing*) Oh no, Nell's the star. She's still at the theatre.
Charles There! Mummy'll be home later! Goodgie goodgie goo!
Louise So, where's my room?
Charles Well, as you can see we're kind of full just at present.

Louise suddenly pouts and stamps and screams like a little kid

Louise But I want my own room! And I want it now!
Duke Calm down! (*He hurriedly explains to Charles*) She's a bit fraught after the journey.
Charles Oh, dear. Poor little Linda.
Louise *Louise!*

Barbara suddenly bursts out of her bedroom door carrying another baby

Barbara Will you keep that noise down? And what's *he* doing here?
Duke Hallo, cousin.
Charles He's your cousin?
Barbara 'Fraid so.

Charles indicates the baby

Charles And who's that?
Barbara I thought you'd never ask. It's your new baby.
Charles Oh no, you don't! (*He indicates little Charlie*) Mine's the one wearing the cool little bootees. I've been keeping careful track of all this.
Barbara This one's yours too.
Charles Oh no, it isn't.
Barbara Oh yes, it is.
All Oh no, it isn't.
Barbara And why isn't it? The first four were. So's this one.
Charles 'Tisn't.
Barbara 'Tis.
All 'Tisn't.

Barbara Oi! Yours or not, you better treat it like your own or I'll — I'll — I'll chuck it off a cliff.

Barbara has gone too far. There is a shocked silence

   I'll do it!
Agatha You've made little Charlie sick.
Barbara So?
Charles You're making big Charlie sick too.
Duke So as I was saying, Charlie, Louise is here with her suitcase all set to move in ...
Barbara Oh? And where's she going to go?

Charles looks from Louise to Barbara and back again

Charles We just got a vacancy!

Charles looks off and clicks his fingers

   The Charladies run on with a suitcase which they plonk beside Barbara. They change the sign from "Barbara's room" to "Louise's room"

Barbara What's this?
All Bye!

Barbara scowls at the Duke

Barbara Well, thanks a lot cousin.

   Barbara takes the suitcase and baby and goes

Louise vamps herself at Charles

Louise This is really nice of you, Charlie. I must think of some special way to thank you.
Charles Wowsie wow! *(To audience)* What a beautiful personality.

   Charles goes off glassy-eyed

Louise So, when do I get to be queen?
Duke Well, not just yet.

Louise goes into tantrum mode

Act II

Louise But, I wanna be queen! Yes I do, yes I do, I do. You promised!
Duke Not in so many words ...
Louise Queen, queen, queen! And then I have Catholic sons who will be king, king, king.
Duke You've got to be a bit more subtle than that, Linda.
Louise *(screaming)* LOUISE!

The Duke goes off with his fingers in his ears. The Queen comes on from the other way

Queen What is going on here?
Louise Who are you?
Queen I am the queen.
Louise But you look pretty healthy.
Queen I am, thank you.
Louise But they told me you were dying. They promised.
Queen Did they really? And who exactly are you?
Louise I am to be the new queen, just as soon as you die. Let me try your spikey hat on.
Queen I'm sorry, but I have no intention of dying just now.
Louise *(screaming)* I want you to die! Go on, get dying!
Queen I see. And do you always get what you want?

Louise suddenly smiles sweetly

Louise Oh, yes. But first I'll get unpacked.

Louise goes into her room with her case. Nell comes on and goes to talk to Little Charlie

Nell Hallo, Little Charlie ... look! Little bootees!
Nell
Queen } *(together)* Awww!
Agatha I made them myself.
Nell *(to the baby)* Isn't Auntie Agatha clever? So who was that other funny lady?
Agatha Louise. And we don't like her.
Queen She seems to have replaced Barbara.
Nell Oh! You must be pleased.
Queen Pleased? I thought Barbara was bad, but this one...!
Agatha *(an impression of Louise doing a tantrum)* I wanna be queen. You promised!
Nell Is that what's she's like?

Queen That's it exactly.
Nell Charlie just can't get it right sometimes, can he?
Queen I'm almost missing Barbara already. She became a complete joke after Charles saw you and your friends make such a fool of her. I wish something like that could happen again.
Nell The girls'd love the chance ——
Agatha — really, really, really ——
Nell — but James thinks we're a threat to national security.
Queen James is a pain, but what if I planned a trip for the whole court to the coast? He won't be there, so he'd never know. Would you do it?
Nell What do you think, Aggs?
Agatha (*chanting happily*) We're going to the seaside! We're going to the seaside!
Nell Just a shame Rose can't come. She's in Newgate Prison.
Queen What for?
Nell Somebody saw her spending the money out of James' purse.
Queen She got her hands on James' money? Why didn't you tell me before? She would have got a medal if I'd known.
Agatha Can you get her out?
Queen Of course. It's one of the perks of wearing a spikey hat.

All go off

Black-out or the front-cloth rises

THE SEASIDE

The Lights come up. The two doors look like bathing-hut doors. The sea is represented by a huge blue cloth held across the back of the stage. It might have bits of weed and stuff stuck to it

Charles and the Queen come on with deckchairs and get settled. The Queen is dressed in her normal clothes

Queen This looks like an empty spot.
Charles Oh, good. I like it nice and peaceful.
Queen (*shouting off inadvertently straight into Charles' ear*) We've found a nice and peaceful place!

Charles is sent rigid with shock

>*Loads of Charladies and Servants come on with beach stuff and set it up all around them creating the scene*

There's quite a bustle and the King and Queen have to raise their voices to speak

You didn't invite anybody else did you?
Charles Me? Oh, no. Perish the thought.

Most of the entourage go

The King and Queen remain. A few Servants stand beside them in case they're needed

Queen So, it's just you and me then.
Charles Absolutely.
Louise (*off*) Oh, coo-ee! Charles! Your little Louise is here!

Charles tries feebly to look innocent and surprised

Charles Well, I wonder who on earth could have possibly invited her?

Louise comes on through one of the doors. She wears an undaring old-fashioned bathing costume. However, she thinks she's flaunting herself. Charles is rather smitten

Louise Oh, Charlie!
Charles Phwoar! I mean, "What an interesting bathing costume".

Louise approaches them. The Queen is completely at ease

Louise There you are, Charlie. Sitting with your dreary old queen.
Charles Whoa! Steady on there!
Queen Don't embarrass her, Charles. Remember she's French, bless her. She probably hasn't got the hang of the language yet. And what a lovely revealing costume she's wearing.
Charles Really? I hadn't noticed.
Louise I put this on specially for you, Charlie. I see your old queen prefers to keep herself covered, but nature has been kind to me and I like people to know.

Charles is grinning admiringly

Charles (*excusing himself to the queen*) And what a beautiful personality too.

During the following, Louise coyly points out her features. Charles shifts about excitedly, but is aware of the Queen watching him

Louise You like my slim ankles, Charlie?
Charles Yes, absolutely. Top drawer. Er — aren't they, dear?
Queen I'm sure they both have beautiful little personalities too.
Louise And do you like the way my hair caresses my naked shoulders, Charles?
Charles Wow, far out, cosmic — isn't it, dear?
Queen Very fetching.
Louise So tell me, Charles, what more could a man want?
Queen How sweet of you to try and to amuse my husband, Linda.
Louise LOUISE!
Queen Whatever. Oh look, Charles, there's a few others come to join us!

Nell, Agatha, Rose, Violet, Annie and Bess, Mercy and others come pouring out of the second door. Some or all of them seem to just be wearing a towel each. The girls with towels turn to Charles, with their backs to audience and open the towels up briefly

Charles's eyes almost burst out of their sockets

Perhaps a few other men could come up behind the King to whoop and whistle

During the following, Louise is horrified as the girls sing and dance behind her

Song 11: The Seaside Special

Girls   Oh, look at the calendar,
                      It's summer once again
                      So let's ignore the frost bite,
                      And let's ignore the rain
                      And though we're all in England
                      We'll pretend that we're in Spain
                      As we all go naked on the beach
Louise (*shouting*) Go away!
Charles (*speaking*) Get out of the way, Linda! You're blocking the view!
Girls (*singing*)   Even if the temp—rature
                      Is minus twenty-four
                      I'll let you look at mine
                      If you let me look at yours
                      It's every bit as funny,

Act II 65

> Though we've seen it all before
> As we all go naked on the beach.
>
> Adam and Eve only ever wore a leaf
> It's written in the holy book
> So don't be such a meanie, rip off that bikini
> And let ev'rybody have a damn good look...

The girls all tug at Louise's costume

Louise runs off screaming

> So whether you're a big boy or whether you're a girl
> Remember every oyster can produce a pearl
> So let it all hang out and give it all a twirl
> As we all go naked on the beach
> Ev'rybody knows that between your head and toes
> You're born just as naked as can be
> So drive away your gloom as you jettison your bloomers
> Then take a skinny in the icy sea...

Instrumental for swimming sequence

The Girls dash off throwing their towels back on stage as they go

Louise appears "In the sea" behind the cloth

Louise (*waving*) Charlie! Look at me swimming, Charlie!
Charles Wow!

The other girls' heads all suddenly appear around Louise

Girls Hi, Charlie!
Charles Now, I'm in heaven.

The girls all duck down again

There is a synchronized swimming routine. Each girl sticks an arm up above the sea-cloth making graceful hand gestures that are all the same. Alternately, it might look funnier if the cloth has small holes in for them to stick their arms through. The arms disappear. Then a set of legs appear and do some synchronized kicking. The legs disappear

There is a short pause

Louise Where did they go?

Finally their heads suddenly appear. Each girl has a mouthful of water and all together they squirt it at Louise. Louise screams

Charles and the Queen laugh themselves silly

The girls' heads disappear again

Louise No, what? No! Get off me! Let go!

Louise is pulled under. There's a brief commotion, the other girls' heads appear cheering and Louise's costume is thrown at Charles

Girls So if you're being looked at by people near and far
Don't be scared to show them exactly who you are
Be proud as you show 'em all your operation scars
As we all go naked on the beach.

Charles applauds wildly as the girls disappear into the sea

All go off laughing, leaving Louise

Louise You can't just leave me here!

A shark fin suddenly comes across the sea at her

Arghhh!

Louise goes off sharpish

The Charladies come on and clear the set and place the two signs on the doors "Charlie's room" sign and "Louise's room" on the other door

A PALACE CORRIDOR

The Charladies, Elsie, Irene and Rita, mop

Irene (*announcing*) A palace corridor, circa 1671 A.D. Enter stage right: one complete git. (*She indicates* R)

James comes on R *and paces the corridor*

Act II

James Where's the king?
Irene Himself? He's out.
James You won't believe what he's gone and done. Ages ago he promised the French he'd become a Catholic but now he says he can't be bothered. They had a secret treaty and everything.
Rita Not much of a secret with you gobbin' off about it.
James I turned Catholic, so why can't he?
Irene He knows the Protestants would lynch him.
James They didn't lynch me.
Elsie That's because they don't give a toss about you, chuck.
Irene And get off my clean floor.

Hortense comes on

The Charladies eye her curiously

Rita Oh-oh. Here comes trouble.
Hortense Where is Charles?
Irene Who's asking?
Hortense I am Hortense Mancini, the most beautiful woman in Italy.
Elsie That's as maybe, but you're in England now, pet.
Hortense I have left my husband, run away from a convent, escaped kidnappers, fled my homeland and now I need the king to help me.
Rita Like I said ... trouble.
Hortense I am not trouble. If Charles is good to me, then there will be peace with France.
Irene But you're Italian!
Hortense It's a complicated story.

Nell comes on with a baby in a blanket

Nell Anyone seen Charlie? I've got a new baby to show him.
Rita Look ... little bootees!
Charladies Aww!
James New baby? I thought I told you to keep away from him!
Nell I called him James.
James Aww! Well, that's all right then, but no more or I'll be cross.

The Queen comes on

Queen Where's Charles? The army needs paying or they will mutiny.

Titus Oates comes on

Titus I need to speak to the king. The Catholic revolution is growing. Blood will flow in the streets.

Charles comes on

Charles Hallo, everyone!
Nell Charlie!

During the following, they all cluster round Charles and start shouting together

Nell You're ignoring your kids ...
Titus Catholic revolution ...
Queen You've run out of money ...
Hortense I need rooms for twenty servants ...
James There will be wars with the French and the Dutch and the Germans ...
Charladies Get off the floor! We've just mopped that ...

Charles ends up crawling out between their legs

Louise comes on

Charles is just about to escape but bumps into Louise as she comes in

Louise (*screaming*) Charles!

Everybody stops shouting

All Uh?
Louise I've decided you're not giving me enough attention.
Charles Another time, Linda.
Louise *Louise!* So, what's more important? Running the country and getting out of debt and avoiding a major European war — or my happiness? Get thinking, king.
All Thing-king-king?
Charles 'Scuse me, everybody. (*To Louise*) Look, I've got rather a lot on at the moment.
Louise Oh, I see. Like that is it? I suppose our five years together counts for nothing?
All You've had five years of *that*?

Charles nods sheepishly

Queen (*sarcastically*) Doesn't time fly when you're having fun?

Louise Be quiet, old queen. And that's another thing, Charles, why am I not the queen yet?

All point at the Queen

All Duh! Because she's the queen.
Charles I made you Duchess of Portsmouth.
Louise I wanna be queen!
Queen In your dreams, honey.
Louise Charles, you heard her! You heard all of them! Send them away, Charles.
Charles You're being ridiculous, Louise ...
Louise *Linda!*
All Linda?
Louise I mean LOUISE! That does it, I'm going. What do you say to that?
Charles What can I say?

Song 12: Life Without You.

The following song is sung with mock sincerity. Louise doesn't know at all how to take it

The song starts slowly. Charles is passed a handkerchief. He dabs his eyes

There are extra backing vocals in italics

   (*singing*)   If you don't want me any more
                             My tears will saturate the floor...

Charles wrings out the handkerchief and lots of water comes out

All	He'll cry so loudly that he'll dislocate his jaw
	Because without you that's life.
Charles	Do I mean nothing more to you?
All	*Life without ya'*
Charles	I can't believe our love is through
All	*Life without ya'*
	He won't forget you for a least a day or two
	Because without you that's ...

The song starts to swing

                      Sha la-la la-la-la la-la-la la-la-la
                      La-la-la la-la-la, life without ya'

	Sha la-la la-la-la la-la-la la-la-la
	La-la-la la-la-la life without ya'
Charles	Each summer day will bring me rain
All	*Life without ya'*
Charles	A smile will only cause me pain
All	*Life without ya'*
Charles	I'll never feel the need to change my socks again
All	Because without you that's life
	Sha la-la la-la-la la-la-la…ooh
Charles	The memories of you I'll keep
All	*Life without ya'*
Charles	Like how you snorted in your sleep
All	*Life without ya'*
	The way your hair looks like the back end of a sheep
	Because without you that's life
	La la la lah …
Charles	I'm begging you,
All	*Hey you*
Charles	Won't you stay?
All	*Please stay*
Charles	For just one day
All	Oh, Baby
	Surely you see that he's so full of misery.
	Isn't he?
	Ah…
Charles	Before you step,
All	*You step*
Charles	Through the door
All	*The door*
Charles	Turn back once more
All	Oh, Baby
	Surely you see, that you and he
	Are destined to be, e-ter-nal-ly
	Together for ever
	And ever and ever
	And ever and ever and ever and ever
	And knowing there's never a chance that you'll ever be free...
Charles	My heart will be a dying rose
All	*Life without ya'*
Charles	My social life will decompose
All	*Life without ya'*
Charles	And ev'ry evening I'll just sit and pick my nose

All	Because without you that's life
Charles	And ev'ry bird will leave the sky
All	*Life without ya'*
Charles	And ev'ry little fish will die
All	*Life without ya'*
Charles	And every cow will raise its tail as I walk by
All	Because without you that's..
	Sha la-la la-la-la la-la-la la-la-la
	La-la-la la-la without you that's life!

Louise finally storms off in a huff followed by everyone, except Nell and Charles

Nell and Charles remain and chat at one side of the stage

Charles Do you know, Nell, being king would be such brilliant fun if it wasn't for Henry the Eighth.

Nell Come off it! You're the one that fancied Louise, you can't blame old Henry for that.

Charles Oh, Louise is nothing. I blame him because he broke away from the Catholic church and ever since then the Catholics have been trying to get back in.

Nell It's not that bad, is it?

Charles It's hotting up. It's got to the point where I'm the only Protestant left in the palace. Catherine's Catholic and then James turned Catholic of course ...

Nell Don't we know! He never shuts up about how Catholic he is.

Charles Then Louise turned up and of course she's Catholic which is why she was practically forced on to me.

Nell You didn't put up much of a fight!

Charles What was the point? Look what happens the minute Louise walks out ——

Hortense walks on with a suitcase and a notice to hang on the door saying "Hortense's room". She heads towards one of the doors

Hortense Hiya, Charlie!

Charles — the most beautiful woman in Italy moves in. Oi, Hortense, you wouldn't just happen to be Catholic would you?

Hortense But of course.

Hortense exits through the door

Charles Surprise, surprise.

Nell You're getting paranoid!
Charles Why not? Have you any idea what pressure I'm under? I'm trying to be the big peace and love man, but if I so much as uttered one Hail Mary, then every Catholic in the land would think it's prot. bashing season and *bang,* the whole of Europe would pile in. It'd be carnage.
Nell Relax, Charlie. After Cromwell, and the plague and the fire, people have had enough misery. They just want to get on with their lives, they don't want to fight.
Charles That's what I thought, but someone's stirring them up.

Titus appears at the other side of the stage from Nell and Charles. His following lines are delivered as thunderous announcements

This next section should be continuous, as one pair of Charladies leaves the next should be arriving

A couple of Charladies, Vera and Pauline, come on and pass Titus

Titus I say to you, there is to be a Catholic revolution in the land.
Vera
Pauline } *(together)* Fancy!
Titus They are plotting to get rid of the king.
Vera
Pauline } *(together)* Fancy!

The Charladies walk on passing Charles and Nell

Vera Those Catholics! Always up to something.
Pauline Fancy killing the king.
Vera As long as they don't make a mess.

Pauline and Vera go off

Charles You hear what people are saying!

Two more Charladies, Ivy and Brenda, come on and pass Titus

Titus I myself overheard the queen planning to poison the king.
Ivy
Brenda } *(together)* Fancy!
Titus Because she's an evil murdering Catholic!
Ivy
Brenda } *(together)* Fancy!

Act II

The Charladies walk on passing Charles and Nell

Ivy Who'd have thought the queen would poison him?
Brenda She's probably got fed up of all his bawdy women.
Ivy At least poison's nice.
Brenda Yeah. Poison doesn't make a mess.

Ivy and Brenda go off

Charles Catherine! She's finally had enough, she's going to poison me!

Two more Charladies, Dot and Connie, come on and pass Titus

Titus James will become the Catholic king. It's a Popish plot.
Dot ⎫
Connie ⎭ (*together*) Fancy.
Titus And then all Protestants will be slaughtered in their beds !
Dot ⎫
Connie ⎭ (*together*) Fancy.

The Charladies walk on passing Charles and Nell

Dot Slaughtered in their beds. That's not nice.
Connie Think of all that extra laundry.

Dot and Connie go off

Charles is rigid with panic

Nell Charlie! Snap out of it. It's only gossip, the queen loves you!
Charles But the whole country's talking about it.

Titus announces smugly to himself

Titus The king's bound to start persecuting Catholics now! I think this calls for a little celebration down the Rose Tavern.

Titus goes

Charles What can I do?
Nell Get a grip! It's nonsense, I'll prove it to you.
Charles How?
Nell I dunno yet. I'll work on it.

Nell goes off one way, as the Queen comes on the other way with a cup of tea

Charles I don't want to be poisoned!
Queen Ah, Charlie. You look troubled so I made you a cup of tea.

Charles looks at it in panic

Queen What's the matter!
Charles You drink it!
Queen Me? But I made it for you.
Charles I don't care. You drink it.
Queen I don't want it.
Charles Drink it.

Queen mystified, takes a slurp. Charles stares at her. The Queen pulls a strained face. Obviously the tea tastes awful

  Hah!
Queen What's up with you?
Charles Just as I thought. Drink it all. ALL! NOW!

The Queen is intimidated. She swallows the tea in one then clutches her throat and grimaces horribly

  Let that be a lesson to you.

Charles stomps off

The Queen regains her composure

Queen (*shouting after him*) You know I can't stand tea without sugar in it.

The Queen walks off mystified

Black-out or ....

The Charladies come on and take the signs off the doors and place a Rose Tavern pub sign next to one of the doors

OUTSIDE THE ROSE TAVERN

The Lights come up, as Violet, Rose. Agatha, Annie and Bess are ejecting Titus from the Tavern

Act II

Violet Come on, Titus, you've had enough.
Titus But there's a Catholic revolution, I tell you.
Twins Will you give it a rest?
Titus But we'll all be ——

The Belles talk along with Titus — they've heard it all before

Titus
Belles } (*together*) — murdered in our beds.
Rose Yeah, yeah.
Agatha Have a nice day.

Mercy approaches

Mercy What's going on?
Violet He's been mouthing off like this all night.
Titus The queen wants to kill the king, I tell you. Overheard her myself, I did.
Violet That's enough. Time for beddy-byes.

Violet pulls back a fist to punch him but Mercy stops her

Mercy Hang on. You say that you overheard the queen?
Rose He never.
Titus I did. In Somerset House. I was there.
Mercy Were you really?

Mercy takes out her cards and starts to shuffle them

Rose I warn you. We have ways of finding out if you're telling the truth.

Titus panics

Mercy Get his hand.

Violet grabs Titus's left hand and prises the fingers open

Titus You wouldn't dare! I'm an Anglican priest. If you rip out my fingernails, you'll all swing for it.
Violet Oh, grow up! You've only got to pick a card.
Titus A card?

Mercy fans her cards out. Violet forces Titus's hand towards them. He picks a card

Violet There! Now pass it over.

Mercy takes the card and looks at it in amazement

Titus Well? What does that tell you?

Mercy thinks briefly

Mercy We owe you an apology.
Violet Eh?
Mercy Let him go. He's our guest.
Titus Quite. So I should be.
Mercy Bess, would you take our friend back inside. Get him a drink.
Bess ⎫ *(together)* ⎧ Why me?
Annie ⎭ ⎩ Why her?
Mercy Just do it, Bess. Compliments of the house.

The Belles look at Mercy as if she has gone nuts. Rose ushers Titus and Bess towards the Tavern door

Twins This way then, Mr Oates.
Titus Eh? Did they talk together?
Mercy No! Now in you go. Annie, you stay here.

Bess and Titus go off through the Tavern door

Rose is holding Titus's wallet

Violet Honestly, Mercy, you've lost your touch. He's a nutter.
Mercy I know that — look, jack of diamonds reversed! There's something really strange about him.

Rose opens the wallet and inspects some papers inside it

Rose I'll say he's strange. He might be an Anglican priest, but according to his papers, our friend Titus Oates has been a Catholic priest too.
Mercy He isn't just warning about the trouble, I'm pretty sure he's the one that's causing it!
Violet Let's kill him.
Mercy No, we need him so that we can convince Charlie that the queen is innocent.
Rose How do we do that?
Mercy Charlie's having dinner at Nell's tonight, right?

Rose Too right. He's scared of eating anywhere near the queen these days.
Mercy Get them both here.
Rose How's that going to help?

Annie suddenly speaks as if Titus is with her

Annie Sit down here, Mr Oates. I'll get you a large brandy.

They all stare at Annie who claps her hand over her mouth sheepishly. Mercy grins

Mercy We're going to do a bit of eavesdropping! Come on.

They all go off

Black-out

INSIDE THE ROSE TAVERN

There is a table at one side of the stage

As the Lights come up, Bess and Titus are at the table. Titus is drinking quite a lot. At the other side are gathered the other Belles. They are watching Annie. Although Bess is in conversation, Annie says everything in unison with her

Titus I tell you, we're all going to be killed by the Catholics.
Twins Killed by the Catholics?
Titus Oh, yes. I can see the signs.
Twins What signs?
Titus There's plenty of signs. You mark my words.
Violet I'm not sure I can take much more of this.

Rose, Nell and Charles come on and join the Belles at the side of the stage

Nell Mercy! What's going on?
Mercy Shh! Sit down and listen to Annie.
Charles What have you heard, Annie?
Mercy No! It's what Bess might hear that's important. Go on, Annie, ask the question!
Twins Tell me again, what's going to happen to the king?
Titus The queen is arranging to have him poisoned.
Twins The queen's going to have him poisoned?
Charles I knew it! It's true!

Nell No, it isn't. She'd never do that.
Charles Why not? Poor Catherine I've driven her to it.
Mercy Shhhh!
Twins How do you know?
Titus I overheard her myself, plotting with the Spanish in Somerset House.
Twins Somerset House?
Charles Somerset House! It could be, she's got rooms there.
Titus And once the king's gone, no Protestant will be safe, even me.

Titus then bursts out laughing. Charles watches him laughing

Charles What's he got to laugh about?
Mercy Annie, can you ask him?
Twins Why are you laughing about being killed?
Titus Because ... (*He looks round to see that no-one is listening to them. He then moves closer to Bess*) I'll tell you if you're nice to me.
Twins In what way have I got to be nice to you?
Rose Oh, no!
Nell Poor Bess.
Violet I'll stop him before he starts, OK, Annie?

Titus whispers in Bess's ear

Twins You made the whole story up?
Charles He made it up? Why?
Twins Why?
Titus Because I hate Catholics and I want the king to get rid of them.
Twins You want the king to get rid of them?
Charles So that's it!
Nell But we'll need proof that he's been lying.
Mercy Ask about Somerset House.
Twins What's Somerset House like?
Titus How should I know? I've never been near the place.
Twins You've never been near the place?
Titus C'mon, we've talked enough. Now let's get friendly.

Titus leads Bess off who glances anxiously back at the others. Unfortunately, the others are in discussion apart from Annie who is sitting alone at the front

Nell You see, Charlie? Catherine has never been trying to poison you.
Charles So she loves me!
Nell Of course.
Mercy What's more, we can prove to everyone it's all been lies.

Act II

Charles How?
Mercy Put him in court. When he says he overheard the queen plotting, just ask him to describe the inside of Somerset House. He won't be able to!
Nell Then everyone will know.
Charles Brilliant! Come on, back to the palace. I'm going to need some help explaining this to Catherine!

They all go, except Annie

Annie is left seated. She suddenly squirms as if she's being molested

Annie Mr Oates! What do you think you're doing?

Violet and Agatha come back

Violet Annie, are you all right?

Annie squirms a lot more

Annie Urgh! Stop that!
Agatha What's the matter with Annie?
Violet Oh no! I'd forgotten about Bess. Hang on, girl, I'm on my way!

Violet strides off rolling up her sleeve and clenching her fist

Annie Oooh! That tickles! That's rather nice. Do that again, a bit further up ... oooooh!

Off stage we hear a smack and a crunch as Violet knocks Titus out in one. Annie suddenly stops and looks disappointed

Violet comes back on blowing on her knuckles. Bess follows her with her clothes in disarray

Violet All right there, Annie?
Twins S'pose so. I was just starting to enjoy that.

Bess and Annie look at each other and giggle

You should be ashamed of yourself!

They all go off

The Charladies with Irene come on to change the scene to the Palace

Vaults. They strike the tavern table and props and bring on the same table as used in the Magic Room, Act I. It has a long cloth to the floor and as in the previous scene, a person is hidden underneath. They place a treasure chest on the table

Irene Just a minute, girls. Listen ...

They all stop to listen.

Helena (*off, very drunkedly*) Charlie Boy — look my way ...

There is a huge splash

Charladies Aw — shame.

The Charladies continue with the scene change

Irene (*explaining to the audience*) Just so's you know, that was old Helena Gwyn. Fell in Chelsea Creek and drowned. Not exactly the biggest event in history, but sad all the same. Anyway, we're skipping on a couple of years to the next scene. It's only short but it tells you a bit about Nell. The Palace Vaults, 1682.

The Charladies exit

PALACE VAULTS

King Charles and the Queen enter and sit at the table

Charles I can't wait to see Nell's face when she sees what I've got for her.
Queen It's an awful lot of money, Charles.
Charles If they hadn't stopped Titus Oates, it could have cost the country a lot more than this. Those girls have stopped a civil war.

Nell comes on

Nell Charlie! Catherine! What did you want?
Charles Nell, this is long overdue, but here it is.
Nell What is it?
Charles Money, Nell. Enough for you and the girls to live like princesses.
Nell But this is a fortune. Talk sense to him, Catherine.
Queen Take it, Nell! Honestly, without you Charles might have had me locked up for poisoning him.
Nell But I thought you were broke?

Act II 81

Charles Hey! What's the point in being king if you can't raise a bit when you need it?
Nell So where did it come from?
Charles It's old army pensions that never got paid.

Nell is horrified

Nell What?
Charles Don't worry. It's been tucked away for a while, so everyone's forgotten about it.
Nell Oh, Charlie, how could you?
Charles What's the matter?
Nell Ever since I was a little girl living with my mother I've known soldiers. We saw them arrive back from wars, we tried to make them welcome and they were good to us. In fact I daresay one of them was my father. How can I accept this money that they should have had?
Charles You make me feel a bit awkward.
Nell I should hope so too. (*She opens the chest and counts out six bags of coins*) Agatha. Violet. Bess. Annie. Rose. Mercy. That's enough.
Charles What about you?
Nell I've got my house and expenses. I've got the jewellery you gave me. I don't want money meant for war heroes. And don't you dare throw it at Hortense or any of the others either.
Charles So what do I do with it?

Nell shuts the chest

Nell It's soldiers' money so do something for them.
Charles Like what?
Nell Build them an old soldiers' hospital. Somewhere to spend their days in dignity. There's a good site in Chelsea — why not get Christopher Wren to design it?
Charles He's a bit pricey.
Queen Listen to her, Charles. Just for once, put your money to something worthwhile!

The Charladies — Irene and Elsie — come on with mops and buckets

Irene Have you finished?
Charles Er, I suppose so.
Nell Chelsea Hospital, Charles, don't forget!
Queen I'll make sure.
Irene Off you go then.

Elsie And take your piggy bank with you.

Charles and the Queen go off with the treasure chest and money. Nell goes the other way

The Charladies face the audience

Irene All right, you've waited long enough. It's time you saw a bit of real talent.

Loads of extra Charladies come on

Song 13: Filth!

It might be desirable to split the Charladies into two groups A and B, then allocate lines as indicated

All	Mop and bucket and mop and bucket and
	Mop and bucket and mop and bucket and...
Chars A	London used to be a decent place
Chars B	Of filth and dirt there wasn't a trace
All	Respectable people felt safe anywhere
Chars A	Now wherever you care to look
Chars B	There's filth
Chars A	And smut
Chars B	And scum
Chars A	And muck
All	And it's only the scrubbers like us that seem to care
	With a mop mop mop and a bucket
	We mop, mop on and on
	With a mop, mop, mop and a bucket
	We're at it — all day long
Chars A	There's filth in the alleyways and filth in the park
Chars B	And filth almost anywhere when it gets dark
All	You can even hear filth next door coming through the wall
Chars A	We've seen filth on the tables and the chairs
Chars B	And filth along the landing and rolling down the stairs
Chars A	So if you haven't seen filth it's a wonder that it missed ya
Chars B	There's even been filth behind the potted aspidistra
All Chars	With a mop, mop, mop and a bucket
	We mop, mop, on and on
	With a mop, mop, mop and a bucket
	We're at it — all day long
Irene (*shouting*)	Come on, everybody!

Act II

All Mop, mop, mop and a bucket
We mop, mop on and on
With a mop, mop, mop and a bucket
We're at it — all day long
Back to work!

All the Charladies, except Irene, go off

Irene hangs the "Charlie's room" sign on one of the doors

Irene And so to the king's bedroom exterior, February 1685. (*She starts to walk off, but then turns and calls the table*) Come on. Back to your cupboard.

The table follows her off stage as before

OUTSIDE THE KING'S BEDROOM. FEBRUARY 1685

Chiffinch and Mrs Chiffinch enter from one side and hurry towards Violet and Agatha, who enter from the other

Mrs Chiffinch There you are! You've got to help! The king's had a big stroke.
Agatha So? He's had thousands of strokes, in fact as well as strokes he's had tickles, pats, rubs, cuddles, hugs and all sorts.
Chiffinch No! A *real* stroke — he's dying! Guard the door.

Chiffinch and Mrs Chiffinch exit through the king's bedroom door

Violet Tell, Nell!

Agatha runs off, as Hortense rushes on followed by Louise and Barbara

Hold it right there.
Hortense Let me in! I'm his favourite.
Louise Shove off, new girl. He's leaving his money to me.
Barbara Why you? I had four of his kids!
Louise He promised me the rings off his fingers.
Hortense But he dumped you two.
Violet You lot make me sick.

Chiffinch hurries on from the king's bedroom door. A Doctor, wearing glasses, sticks his head round the door

Doctor More leeches! He still has too much blood.

He disappears

Chiffinch Out of the way.

Chiffinch rushes off

Louise tries to push past Violet

Louise I'm going in.
Violet No, you don't.
Louise But, I'm the mother of one of his children.
Barbara So am I.
Hortense Women who've had his children should be allowed to see him.
Violet There isn't room for a grandstand.

Chiffinch rushes back on with a jar

Chiffinch Gangway! Leeches coming through.
All Urghhh!

They all leap aside

Chiffinch goes through the bedroom door

The door shuts

Violet You may as well leave. Nell's the only one that's getting in. You people are trash.
Hortense How dare you?
Violet Nell's never had another boyfriend since she met Charlie.
Barbara None?
Violet None. And which of you moneygrabbers can say that?

They all look a bit sheepish

Louise Come on, we're wasting our time.

They start to move off

Nell dashes on

Barbara Oh, look! Here comes Little Miss Faithful.
Hortense There's no rush.
Louise He wouldn't die without seeing his true love.

Nell True love? You've never understood him have you? There's only one woman he's ever loved.
All Who?

The door opens

The Queen is ushered out by Mrs Chiffinch

Nell (*to Violet*) Get them out before the queen sees them.
Barbara I'd like to see you try.
Violet My pleasure.

Violet socks Barbara on the jaw. Barbara falls backwards to be caught by Louise and Hortense

They hurriedly drag her off

Mrs Chiffinch You must take a rest.
Queen I won't leave him. I won't.
Mrs Chiffinch You've not slept for forty-eight hours.

The Doctor sticks his head round the bedroom door

Doctor Get the branding irons! Quick!

Chiffinch dashes out of the door and off

Queen Branding irons?
Doctor I assure you, madam, we are applying some of the most technically advanced medical ideas known to man.
Queen So far you've blistered him, flushed him out with scalding water, attached leeches and now you're branding him?
Doctor No. Now, I'm going to shave his head. Then I brand him.
All Urgh!
Doctor Trust me, I'm a doctor.

The Doctor goes back through the bedroom door with Mrs Chiffinch

Nell How are you?
Queen Nell! It's good of you to come.
Nell Is there anything we can do?

Chiffinch returns with a towel wrapped round his hands and holding hot branding irons

Chiffinch Owww...! Out of the way...

Chiffinch goes through the bedroom door

Nell What the hell are you doing to him?

The Doctor looks out. He is wielding a huge nasty-looking carpenter's saw and a blood-stained towel

Doctor We are making him comfortable.

The Doctor shuts the door

All Comfortable?

There is a massive scream from Charles from behind the door. The Queen weeps. Nell comforts her

Queen Do you know what he said to me? He said, "I'm sorry for being such a long time dying." He says that *he's* sorry...
Nell He's supposed to be the Merry Monarch. He should spend his last hours laughing.
Queen You could always make him laugh, Nell.
Nell Remember when we all turned up on the beach?
Violet Shame we can't do something like that again.
Queen Why not?
Nell They wouldn't allow it.
Queen Oh wouldn't they? This sounds like a job for Spikey Hat girl. Come on.

Black-out

INSIDE THE KING'S DEATHCHAMBER

The Lights rise on King Charles in his bed. There is what looks like an inflated purple balloon, full of liquid, sticking out of the king's arm. It's about the size of an apple. There is a chair and table beside the bed. The Doctor and Nurse look on. The Nurse has a bag

Doctor How are the leeches doing, Nurse?
Nurse That's the last one.

The Nurse plucks the bloated balloon from the king's arm. Charles groans.

Act II

She passes it to the doctor who casually tosses it from hand to hand

Doctor Hungry little fella, aren't you? You've been busy.
Nurse You've been busy too, Doctor.
Doctor Yes indeed. It's been a long day.

The Doctor puts the "leech" down, then removes his glasses and puts them down next to it. He rubs his eyes

Nurse You look tired, Doctor. When did you last eat?
Doctor Eat? How can I eat at a time like this?
Nurse A time like what?
Doctor A time like when I have no food.
Nurse Have this apple. (*She takes an apple out of her bag and puts it next to the leech*)
Doctor Thank you.

Ho, ho, you can see what's coming can't you? The doctor reaches for the apple, but without his glasses his eyesight is terrible. His hand scrabbles along and picks up the leech

Doctor Ah! The apple. (*He is about to bite it*) Soft and juicy. My favourite.
Nurse NO! (*She swaps the apple for the leech at the last second*)
Doctor Aha! That's better. (*He takes a bite*)

The Nurse stands very close to him admiringly

  Tomorrow, I think I shall bang some nails into his skull.
Nurse Isn't that very painful?
Doctor You're right. The last time I did it I hit my thumb with the hammer. It was agony.

The Nurse stands face to face with the Doctor

Nurse Gosh, you're so devoted
Doctor You're devoted too.
Nurse You're wonderful.
Doctor You're wonderful too.

The Nurse holds the Doctor's glasses to his face

Nurse Your spectacles.
Doctor You're spectacles too.

The Nurse puts the Doctor's glasses on him

Doctor Time to go then. Make sure the patient is not disturbed by anyone. You understand?
Nurse Yes, Doctor.
Doctor Very good.

The Doctor turns to go

Nurse Good-night, Doctor
Doctor Night, Nurse.
Nurse Yes, Doctor?

The Doctor turns back

Doctor What?
Nurse I thought you wanted something. You said, "Night, Nurse" and I'm the Night Nurse.
Doctor No — not *Night* Nurse, I meant night, Nurse.
Nurse Oh.
Doctor Well, night, Night Nurse.
Nurse Night night, Doctor.

The Doctor goes

The Nurse tries to settle into a chair. She can't, so she grabs a pillow from under Charles' head and roughly pulls it out. Charles groans in agony. She puts it on her chair then settles comfortably

The door opens

The Queen comes in. She is followed by Nell, and all the girls. They are all dressed in long doctor coats

Nurse What's going on?
Queen This is the evening shift. They're going to work on the king through the night.
Charles (*weakly*) Oh, no!
Nurse Are they all doctors?

The girls all reply in normal girl voices

Girls Yes, we are.

Charles Argh!
Nurse They sound like girls.

The girls reply in very deep voices

Girls No, we're not.
Queen You're tired. Your ears are playing tricks on you. Go, take a rest.
Nurse Suits me.

The Nurse goes

The Queen and the girls all gather round Charles. The Queen flexes her fingers menacingly

Charles Please! What are you going to do?
Queen This ...

Song 14. Gimme the Nurse

The Queen holds out her hands to mime playing the guitar as the opening riff to the song starts

Queen	When they say you're looking better but you're feeling really ill
	The relatives are waiting to read the will
	The chaplain calls, gives you grace
	And the undertaker measures you just in case
	You shout:
All	Doctor — I'm a-going down
	Doctor — you needn't stick around
Nell	I'm feeling bad
Rose	You're making it worse
Twins	I don't want a doctor ——
All	Gimme the Nurse!

Brief instrumental as girls throw open their coats to reveal 1960's style saucy nurse uniforms. The Queen keeps her doctor's coat

Charles struggles to sit up. He is clearly gobsmacked

All	Doctor ——
Queen	Who me?

All	— You tried everything
	Doctor —
Queen	You mean me?
All	— He'll soon be growing wings
Queen	I'm sorry.
All	He's feeling bad and you're making it worse
	He don't want a doctor ...
Charles	Gimme the nurse!
All	Give him a nurse — give him a nurse
	The nurse is clean and warm and nice
	But the doctor's hands are cold like ice
	The nurse makes ev'rything all right
	When she tucks you in and says sleep tight
Queen	When they put in a bed that's on the bottom floor
	So they don't have to carry you far no more
Twins	When your long lost friends all write you a letter
All	You can bet that you ain't getting better
	So doctor — I beg you no more tricks
	Doctor — he feels a hundred and six
	He's feeling bad and you're making it worse
	He don't want a doctor...
Charles	Gimme the nurse!

Instrumental

All	The nurse is fun and the nurse is smart
	And most of all the uniform's a work of art
	But behind the smile it's well worth knowing
	When the going gets tough, the nurse gets going
	Doctor — he's a-going down
	Doctor — you needn't stick around
	He's feeling bad
	You're making it worse
	He don't want a doctor
Agatha	Nothing personal
All	He don't want a doctor
Mercy	Stick your medicine
All	He don't want a doctor no more.
	Give him a nurse!
Charles	Oh, yeah!

James rushes on with a priest, Father Huddlestone, and a Guard or two

Act II

James Charles, I'm here, I'm ready! Pass that crown over and let's get ruling! Hey what are this lot doing here?
Queen They are looking after Charlie.
James Oh no, not Nell's Belles! Charles, is this how you think a king should die?
Charles It seemed pretty good to me.
James For God's sake! I've got Father Huddlestone here to see you. What's he going to think?
Father (*happily admiring the girls*) Oh, I'm absolutely appalled.
James Arrest them. Take them away. Lose them, bury them. In the meantime Charles, you've just got time to become a Catholic before you die.

The Guards advance on the girls

Charles No way, James.
James But you promised.
Charles You let the girls go.
James Never! I told you after the fire and I'm telling you now, if word of "Nell's Belles" gets out, it could ruin the reputation of the whole monarchy. It's all right for you. You'll be dead in a few hours. I've got to be king remember.
Charles I'll only be Catholic if you let them go. Catherine, Father, you're witnesses.

James approaches the girls

James Listen well, "Nell's Belles". I never want to hear that name again. "Nell's Belles" will be struck from any public record, deleted from history books and anyone passing the name by word of mouth shall lose their tongue. From now on, "Nell's Belles" has never existed. Now get out.

The girls, except Nell, all go

Nell lingers

Nell Charlie ...
James GO.

Nell weeps and goes

Queen comes to hold Charles' hand

Queen Are you ready for the priest?

Charles Bring him on. Anyone's better than that doctor.
Father Good-oh. Never too late to be a Catholic that's what I say.
James Get on with it.
Father Funny, isn't it? Your first Catholic service is going to be the last rites. First, last — you've got to laugh, haven't you? Off we go then. (*He makes the sign of the cross as he starts*) *Per sacrosancta humanae reparationis mysteria* ... (*He continues softly with the following under James and Charles*) ... *remittat tibi omnipotens. Deus omnes praesentis et futurae vitae poenas, paradisi portas aperiat, et ad gaudia, sempiterna perducat.* Amen.
Charles James!
James What?
Charles Another thing. Let not poor Nelly starve.
James But she's just an actress! Do you really expect me to give her a pension and——
Charles Shhh.(*He indicates to James to be quiet as Father Huddlestone continues with the rites*)

Companies may either do both prayers or just the following prayer, in place of the first

Father *Ego, facultate mihi ab Apostolica sede tributa, indulgentiam plenariam et remissionem omnium peccatorum tibi concedo. In nomine Patris, et Filii,* (*He makes the sign of the cross*) *et Spiritus Sancti.* Amen.

The front-cloth falls or Black-out

THE PALACE GARDENS

The Lights come up

Nell enters and is weeping. After a few seconds Charles bounds on looking as well as ever

Nell is astonished

Charles Nell, baby!
Nell Charlie?
Charles Thank goodness that's over with.
Nell What's over?
Charles Dying. I tell you, Nell, that was painful.
Nell So you're alive?

Act II 93

Charles No! I'm dead. Ha! No backing out of that one I can tell you. When the priest sends you up, then up you gotta go. Catch the express to cloud city and all that.
Nell So how can I see you?
Charles Questions, questions! Now listen, I've arranged for James to pay all your bills and everything.
Nell James?
Charles He's not too happy about it, so he'll probably sneak it out of the secret service fund.
Nell Thanks, Charlie.
Charles No, thank you, Nell. The sixties and seventies were tough, but you and the girls kept me going.
Nell Those were amazing years to live in.
Charles It was a truly groovy time, and you know what? One day we're going to meet up and do it all again.
Nell What do you mean, Charlie?

Charles turns to walk off and beckons Nell to follow

Black-out

The Lights come up or the front-cloth rises

Mr and Mrs Chiffinch are in 60s' disc jockey gear

THE SIXTIES

Chiffinch It's Saturday, it's sunny and it's sixty-three.
Mrs Chiffinch The forecast is sun, sun, sun, and fun, fun, fun.
Chiffinch That's right so get your feet with the beat and pile on your nylons.
Mrs Chiffinch Here come a few old favourites to clear the static out your attic.
Chiffinch Ready for this you cool cats?
Both Then let's party!

Song 15: The Happiest Days (reprise)

Everyone comes on dressed in groovy 60s' clothes, singing ...

All (*singing*)   Do you remember back in sixty-four?
I'd never tried to make a move before
I wanted to kiss you, you told me I could,
Since then I never had a lovin' so good.

You always told me that you didn't care,
Just coincidence you're always there,
You made me so glad when you were able to stay,
I had a mouth full of words but with nothing to say.

Kids of the Sixties
They'll never know
The gloom of the Fifties
So long ago
They tell us that we've never had it so good
They tell us that we've never had it so good
These are the happiest days of our lives.

Every single morning brings a better day
Every single dance'll blow the night away
Summer and autumn, winter and spring
Every day has a treasure to bring.

Ev'ry body party till we hit the top
Nobody can tell us that we've got to stop
We're coming out like a shot from a gun
Young and single, ready for fun
Kids of the Sixties
They'll never know
The gloom of the Fifties
So long ago
They tell us that we've never had it so good
They tell us that we've never had it so good
These are the happiest days of our lives.

Instrumental

If possible, Nell and Charles come on either on a scooter or some sort of "car" with "Charlie" and "Nell" written on the windowscreen

Happiest days of our lives.

Black-out

The Lights come up for the cast to take their curtain calls. Possibly with the "Table" making an appearance

Act II

Reprises of other songs as required. You may wish to finish with:

Song 16: The Seaside Revisited

All (*singing*) Oh, what a tragedy —the show's about to end
But the party's hardly started, so go and grab a friend
And join us on a trip that we can really recommend
As we all go naked on the beach.

If you're posh or penniless we really couldn't care
A great big smile is all you need to wear
So let the water sprinkle ev'ry wrinkle if you dare
As we all go naked on the beach
You've sat in the gloom of the same stuffy room
So long you've all gone numb
So give your circulation a quick rejuvenation
And get a bit of ventilation round that bum
So if you're being boring, get yourself to bed
And ev'rybody else can come with us instead
If you're shy of what you've got then you might as well
  be dead
As we all go naked on
We all go naked on
We all go naked on the beach.

Huge applause

Please note that the author takes absolutely no responsibility for any of the following stage direction:

  Streakers and swarms of press photographers with flash bulbs going off come on

Cheers

  Police arrive with blue flashing lights

There are shrieks of laughter and general pandemonium

However, he hopes that you'll all be bailed out in time for the next performance

The CURTAIN *falls*

FURNITURE AND PROPERTY LIST

ACT I

On stage: One or two theatrical items — laundry baskets, odd boxes
Two doors. *On them*: star and sign reading "Wardrobe"

Off stage: Bottle containing liquid (**Helena**)
King's severed head (**Stage management**)
Large, bright handkerchief (**Hart**)
Some bits of paper, notebook and pen (**Duncan**)
Crown-shaped door sign reading "Charlie's room" (**Charladies**)
Door sign on string reading "Do Not Disturb" (**Charladies**)
Tray of teacups (**Mr and Mrs Chiffinch**)
Tennis racket (**Charles**)
Mop and bucket (**Irene**)
Bow and arrow (**Queen**)
Mops and buckets (**Rita and Elsie**)
Chamber pot containing confetti (**Elsie**)
Rose Tavern pub sign (**Charladies**)

Personal: **Mercy**: pack of cards (needed throughout)
Rose: snuff-box, money, penknife and pocketbook

During black-out on page 24

Strike: Tavern door sign

Set: Table with long cloth. *On it*: deck of cards
Oil lamps and candles

Off stage: Royal box (**Charladies**)
Baskets of oranges (**Belles**)
Bar stools, tables, drinks (**Charladies**)
Hand-bell (**Reaper**)
Cart (**Spooky figures**)
Baker's counter, food, candles (**Charladies**)
Stage magazine (**Chiffinches**)
Several newspapers (**Newspaper sellers**)
A note (**Mercy**)
Tray of pies and other eats (**The Baker**)
Fire extinguishers (**Charladies**)

Furniture and Property List 97

Personal: **Queen**: coins
Charles: beard in pocket

ACT II

On stage: Rows of cathedral-type seating

Off Stage: Selection of brushes, dusters, buckets (**Irene, Elsie and Rita**)
Crown-shaped sign reading "Charlie's room" (**Charladies**)
Heart-shaped sign reading "Barbara's room" (**Charladies**)
Showbiz magazine (**Mrs Chiffinch**)
Toothbrush (**Charles**)
Dressing-room chairs, mirror, door signs to stars (**Charladies**)

Personal: **Rose**: purse

During the black-out on page 58

Strike: Dressing-room setting

Set: Signs on doors: "Charlie's room" and "Barbara's room"

Off stage: Clipboards (**Mr and Mrs Chiffinch**)
Suitcase (**Duke**)
Baby (**Agatha**)
Baby (**Barbara**)
Suitcase, sign reading "Louise's room" (**Charladies**)

During the black-out on page 62

Strike: Signs on doors

Set: Huge blue sea cloth. *On it*: weeds and other bits

Off stage: Two deckchairs (**King and Queen**)
Beach stuff (**Charladies and Servants**)
Towels (**Belles and Girl chorus**)
Shark fin (**Stage Management**)
Two bedroom door signs — "Charlie's room" and "Louise's room"
   (**Charladies**)
Mops (**Charladies**)
Baby in blanket (**Nell**)
Handkerchief with trick water squeezer (**Member of chorus**)
Suitcase, notice reading "Hortense's room" (**Hortense**)
Cup of tea (**Queen**)
Rose Tavern pub sign (**Charladies**)

Personal: **Rose**: **Titus**'s wallet containing papers

During black-out on page 77

Strike: *Rose Tavern* pub sign

Set: Tavern table and chairs. *On it*: drinks

Off stage: Table with long cloth (**Charladies**)
Treasure chest containing money (**Charladies**)
Mops and buckets (**Irene and Elsie**)
"Charlie's room" door sign (**Irene**)
Jar (**Mr Chiffinch**)
Towel and hot branding irons (**Mr Chiffinch**)
Huge nasty-looking carpenter's saw and blood-stained towel (**Doctor**)

During black-out on page 86

Strike: Room door signs

Set: The **King Charles**'s bed, with pillows
Apple sized purple balloon, full of liquid, for **Charles**'s arm
Chair and table
Bag for **Nurse**

Off stage: Scooter or car for **Nell** and **Charles** (see description page 94)

If required

Cameras with flash bulbs (**Press photographers**)

LIGHTING PLOT

Practical fittings required: oil lamps, camera flash bulbs

Act I

To open: Darkness

Cue 1	Sound of single drum beat; distant crowd murmurs When ready, bring up lighting DS	(Page 1)
Cue 2	**Helena** and the **Barmaid** exit *Black-out*	(Page 3)
Cue 3	The musical introduction for Song No 1 begins *Bring up lighting*	(Page 3)
Cue 4	**Violet** ushes **Helena** off *Black-out*	(Page 24)
Cue 5	When ready *Bring up dim spooky lighting, practical oil lamps, covering spots on candles*	(Page 24)
Cue 6	**Irene** exits *Black-out*	(Page 28)
Cue 7	The **Belles** enter *The lights come up DS, follow spots in auditorium*	(Page 28)
Cue 8	The **Belles** come on to the stage *Cut follow spots in auditorium*	(Page 30)
Cue 9	**Hart** and **Nell** exit *Bring up full lighting*	(Page 33)
Cue 10	**Mercy** "We've got DEATH!" *The lights dim*	(Page 35)
Cue 11	**Agatha and Belles** return to position before song *Revert to previous cue*	(Page 37)

Cue 12	The **Charladies** enter quietly *The lights cross fade* DS	(Page 38)
Cue 13	**Mr** and **Mrs Chiffinch** go *The lights fade to black-out*	(Page 40)
Cue 14	When ready *Bring up general lights and covering spotlights on candles in Baker' shop scene*	(Page 40)
Cue 15	**Charles** makes his way to sit in the auditorium *Bring up follow spotlight on* **Charles**	(Page 43)
Cue 16	**Charles** makes his back to the stage *Fade spotlight*	(Page 45)
Cue 17	**Charles** and **Nell** knock over a candle and go *Flickering orange fire effect increasing in intensity*	(Page 46)
Cue 18	The **Charladies** come on; when ready *Black-out*	(Page 46)

ACT II

To open: General lighting

Cue 19	**Mercy**: " ... from a pregnancy test?" *Black-out*	(Page 58)
Cue 20	When ready *Bring up lights* DS	(Page 58)
Cue 21	**All** exit *Black-out*	(Page 62)
Cue 22	The front-cloth rises *Bring up full general lighting*	(Page 62)
Cue 23	The **Queen** walks off, mystified *Black-out*	(Page 74)
Cue 24	Set change; when ready *Bring up full general lights*	(Page 74)
Cue 25	The **Belles** all go off *Black-out*	(Page 77)

Lighting Plot

Cue 26	Set change; when ready *Bring up full general lights*	(Page 77)
Cue 27	**Queen**: "Come on." *Black-out*	(Page 86)
Cue 28	Set change; when ready *Bring up full general lighting*	(Page 86)
Cue 29	**Father**: "... *et Spiritus Sancti.* Amen." Black-out	(Page 92)
Cue 30	Set change; when ready *Bring up full general lighting*	(Page 92)
Cue 31	**Charles** turns to walk off and beckons **Nell** to follow *Black-out*	(Page 93)
Cue 32	Scene change or the front-cloth rises *Bring up full general lighting*	(Page 93)
Cue 33	At the end of Song 15 *Black-out*	(Page 94)
Cue 34	When ready *Bring up full general lighting*	(Page 94)

If required

Cue 36	Swarms of **press photographers** come on *Activate camera flash bulbs*	(Page 95)
Cue 37	**Police** arrive *Blue flashing lights*	(Page 95)

EFFECTS PLOT

ACT I

Cue 1	To open *Slow single drum beat. Distant crowd murmurs*	(Page 1)
Cue 2	**Soldiers**: "Off in one ..." Pause *Huge cheer*	(Page 2)
Cue 3	**James** leans at the side of the stage *Small hand-bell tinkles*	(Page 17)
Cue 4	**James** hurriedly steps aside *Small hand-bell tinkles*	(Page 17)
Cue 5	**Rita** shoos **James** off stage *Small hand-bell tinkles*	(Page 17)
Cue 6	**Queen**: "'Big Babs'"? *Bell tinkles angrily*	(Page 18)
Cue 7	**Belles**: " ... chuck something..." *Fanfare and an audience cheer*	(Page 29)
Cue 8	**Rose**: " But has he brought her?" *Audience booing*	(Page 29)
Cue 9	**Barbara** tries to wave at the audience *Audience booing increases*	(Page 29)
Cue 10	At the end of Song No. 5 *Big audience cheer*	(Page 30)
Cue 11	**Barbara** runs off *Shouts of derision*	(Page 30)
Cue 12	Stage is lit with flickering orange lighting *Optional Smoke effect*	(Page 46)

Effects Plot

ACT II

Cue 13　**Helena** and **Mercy** enter. Pause　(Page 55)
　　　　Audience applause

Cue 14　**Annie**: " a bit further up ... oooooh!"　(Page 79)
　　　　Smack and crunch sound of **Violet** *knocking* **Titus** *out*

Cue 15　**Helena**: " ... look my way ..."　(Page 80)
　　　　Huge splash

www.ingramcontent.com/pod-product-compliance
Ingram Content Group UK Ltd.
Pitfield, Milton Keynes, MK11 3LW, UK
UKHW021839210426
5322IPUK00022B/374